Distribution list for Alberta

Canada. Post Office Dept.

DISTRIBUTION LIST FOR ALBERTA

CONTAINING

1. The names of the Post Offic alphabetically arrang d.

2. Showing the distribution of the different po: office .c . ndpoint e. t Willi (See page 2).

3. The name of the Postal Car Routes, Section of Pos al Car Route or Di s through which matter for the several offices should pass

4. The names of the Offices to which the matter is forwarded by he Railway Mail Dis-tributing Offices when not mailed direc . (Direct Mails are indicated b dotted line)

5 The names of the Mail Routes by which the offices are served whe n not situa f Railway. When an office served by two or more route the hou o parture fr l terminal points are giver

INSTRUCTION

1. Matt for any office which is supplied by more than one r ut should be or one by whi h it will most speedily reach its destination.

2. When any doubt exists as to the proper railway rout by whi h matter should pplication should be made to the Superintendent, Railway Mail Serv ce. Similar info d be obtained from the P Office Inspector regarding Mail Routes he of Railwa

3. Offices newly bli hed, and Office to whi h new ould be n the List of Offices h the same initial letter. To the entries under e ould be pr onsecutive numbers which numbers should be neatly in ed in heir n the General L n which the names of the n w Offices or the new nam of the old Off ould, in pro he numbering should be from one upwards in each letter.

4 In of the f name, the old name should be d li and *han ed to* . . . . (the new nam w oppo e to er sure. Opposite the n of the w name should be writt forme ly . . . ." (the old name).

5 It is the duty of Superintendents of Railw Mail and P ers *personally* that the Distribution Books furnished to each clerk under their super n are corrected from lists issued from the Post Office Department and the Offic of the ntroll R. M. wa

Post Office Department,
Office of Controller R. M. S.

Ottaw 26th Jany., 1916

KEY TO EAST OF FORT WILLIAM STANDPOINT SCHEME

1. W. M. J. R. P. O.
1a. Portage la Prairie Dis
1b. Macgregor & Dis
1c. Carberry & Dis
1d. Virden & Dis
1f. Qu'Appelle Dis
1g. Regina Dis
1h. Moose Jaw Dis
2d. Humboldt Dis
3b. Napawa Dis.
3d. [illegible] R.P.O.
3e. [illegible] Dis
6a. [illegible] Dis
8a. Ft. F. & W. R.P.O.
8b. Selkirk & Dis
8c. Stonewall & Dis
8d. E. & W. R.P.O.
9. B. & [illegible] R.P.O.
10. Brandon Dis
11. [illegible] R. R.P.O.
11a. R. & W. R.P.O.
12a. S. R. [illegible] P.O.
12b. Swan River & Dis
13. B. & [illegible] R.P.O. No. 1
14. [illegible] B. & [illegible] R.P.O.
14a. Battleford Dis
14b. North Battleford Dis
14c. C. & L. R.P.O.
15. R. & P. A. [illegible] 1.
15. [illegible] R.P.O. Alberta
16. M. P. & M. J. R.P.O.
16. [illegible] R.P.O.
17. M. J. & C. R.P.O.
17a. Maple Creek & Dis
18. M. H. & N. R.P.O.
18b. Edmonton Dis
19. [illegible] Cal. R.P.O.
20. [illegible] R.P.O.
21a. [illegible] R. [illegible] R.P.O.
22. [illegible] & W. in. East of Sask.
22a. [illegible] & W. [illegible] West of Sask
22b. [illegible] Ed. R.P.O.
23. M. J. [illegible] C. R.P.O.
24. [illegible] & H. R.P.O.
24a. Markham Dis
24b. R. [illegible] Mel. R.P.O.
26. [illegible] Mu. & [illegible] R.P.O.
27. Red. [illegible] M. J. R.P.O.
28. [illegible] & [illegible] R.P.O.
29. [illegible] & Mack. R.P.O.
30. [illegible] P. G. R.P.O. No. 1
30a. [illegible] P. G. R.P.O. No. 2

SCHEDULE showing names of Railways from which Post Offices in Alberta are served, the terminal points of the several Postal Car routes, or sections of Postal Car routes on these railways, and the abbreviations by which these terminal points are designated in the following Distribution List. (The names of Railway Post Offices are given in all cases from East to West and from South to North.)

Abbreviations in Distribution List.	Name of Railway.	Terminal Routes between which Postal Cars run.	
C. & E.	Canadi .n Pacific Ry.	algary	Edmonton.
C. & L.......	" "	oronation	Lacombe.
C. & V......	" "	algar	Vancouver.
Ed. & P. G.	Grand Trunk Pacific Ry	dmonton.	Pr. George
H. & W...	Canadi . Pacific Ry.	ard	Wetaskiwin.
Mac. & Cal..	Can. . n Pacific Ry	Macleod	Calgary.
M. H. & N..	" "	Medi e I	Nelson.
M. J. & C..	"	Moo Jaw	Calgary.
Mun. & Cam.	. n Northern Ry	Mun m..	Camrose.
N. B. & E.		. Battleford.	Edmonton.
Wat. & W..n..	Grand Trunk Pacific R	W	Wainwright.
S. & C..	Canad. n Northern Ry		Calgary
S. & H...	Canadi .n Pacific Ry.	..skatoon	Hardisty.
W. & E.	Grand .unk Pacific R.	.ainwri	Edmonton.
S. C. & Emp	CPR	Swift Cur	Empress

OFFICE	KEY No.	COUNTY	DISTRIBUTION
		Bow R.	

ALBERTA DISTRIBUTION LIST

The first column under the Head "Distribution" shows the Postal Car Route or Distributing Office through which Mail matter for the several Offices should pass. The second column under the head "Distribution" shows the Office on which Mail matter is forwarded by the Railway Mail Clerk or Distributing Office when not mailed direct. The third column gives the frequency and other necessary particulars regarding the service. Dy.* means daily including Sunday. Dy. means daily except Sunday. The letters (S.) & (W.) following the name of the forward Office show how the matter should be forwarded in Summer and Winter respectively. A* before the name of an Office, indicates that it is a Customs Port or Out port, and (S.) after the name of an Office indicates a Summer Office

Office	Key No	County	Distribution		
Abilene	14	Victoria	N. B. & E.	Lamont	Saddle Lake, Tue Sat. 14.00.
Acadia Valley	15f	Med. Hat.	[illegible]S. & C.	Alsask	Tue Fri. 10.00.
Acme	17c	Calgary	Calgary		Dy. tr. 630, C.P.R.
Aden	18a	Med. Hat.	Lethbridge	Coutts	St. Kilda, Wed. 7.00.
Aetna	18a	Med. Hat.	Lethbridge	Cardston	Tue. Sat. 14.00.
Airdrie	17	Calgary	C. & E. (No. 1)		Dy. trs. 523, 524, 525, 526
Albeck	17	Med. Hat.	M. J. & C.	Coleridge	Gros. Ventre, Fri. 17.00
Albert Park	17c	Calgary	Calgary		Dy. 8.00.
Albion Ridge	18a	Med. Hat.	Calgary Lethbridge	Noble Ford	T. T. S. 14.45.
Alderson	17	Med. Hat.	M. J. & C.		Dy. trs. 3, 4.
Aldersyde	19	Macleod	Mac & Cal. Calgary		Dy. trs. 537-540. Dy. tr. 538 C.P.R.
Alhambra	20	Red Deer	Red Deer		M. W. F. tr. 613 C.P.R.
Alix	14d	Red Deer	C. & L.		Dy. trs. 529, 530.
Allerston	18a	Med. Hat.	Lethbridge	Milk River	Tue. Fri. 14.00.
Altorado	18a	Med. Hat.	Lethbridge	Warner	Tue. Fri. 7.00.
Amethyst	17	Med. Hat.	Suffield Sta.	Lomond	Kinmondale, Tue. Sat. 18.10.
Amisk	24	Strathcona	S. & H.		Dy. trs. 51, 52.
Andrew	14	Victoria	N. B. & E.	Lamont	Mon. Thu. 7.00.
Angle Lake	14	Victoria	Vermilion		Tue. Fri. 13.00.
Anning	14	Victoria	Vegreville	Duvernay	Tue. 8.00.

OFFICE	KEY No	COUNTY	DISTRIBUTION		

OFFICE	KEY No.	COUNTY	DISTRIBUTION		
Anselmo	21	Edmonton	Edmonton	Green Court	Thur. 13.30.
Ardenode	15f	Calgary	S. & C.		M. W. F. tr. 24 T. T. S. tr. [illegible]
Ardenville	18	Macleod	Macleod	Wellsville	Wed. Sat. 13.30.
Ardley	17c	Red Deer	Calgary		Dy. tr. 11 G. T. P.
Ardmore	14	Victoria	Vegreville	St. Paul de Metis	Durlingville, Wed. 7.00.
Ardrossan	22b	Victoria	W. & E.		Dy. Tr. 2.
Armada	17c	Med. Hat	Calgary Lethbridge	Vulcan	Mon. Thur [illegible]
Arrowwood	17c	Macleod	Calgary Lethbridge	Vulcan	Tue. Sat [illegible]00.
Arvilla	21	Edmonton	Edmonton	Busby	Tue., Fri. [illegible]
Ashmont	14	Victoria	Vegreville	Duvernay	[illegible] 8.00.
Aspen Beach	20	Red Deer	Lacombe		Dy. 8.00.
*Athabaska	21	Edmonton	Edmonton		M. W. F. tr. [illegible] N.R.
Atlee	17	Med. Hat	Bassano. Empress.		Mon. [illegible] 670 C.P.R. Mon. Th. tr. 671 C.P.R.
Auburndale	14	Strathcona	Vermilion		Tues. Fri. 8.00.
Avalon	18a	Med. Hat	Lethbridge	Warner	Altorado, W[illegible]

Sup. Guide June 1918

Office	Key No.	County	Distribution		

Office	Key No.	County	Distribution		
Badger Lake	17	~~Med. Hat~~	~~Suffield Sta.~~	Lomond.	Tue. Sat. 14.00.
Ballantine	21	Edmonton	Edmonton	Cherhill	Wed. Sat. 13.30.
Balermo	17c	Red Deer	Calgary / Edmonton	Delburne	Tue. Sat. 7.00.
Balham	14	Victoria	Fort Sask'n	Redwater	Fri. 16.00.
Balm	21	Edmonton	Edmonton	Green Court	Thur. 13.30.
*Banff	17	Calgary	C. & V. (No. 1)	...	Dy.* trs. 3, 4, 1, 2.
Bankhead	17	Calgary	C. & V. (No. 1)	..	Dy. trs. 3, 4, 1
Baraca	15f	Med. Hat	S. & C.	Stanmore.	Berry Creek. Mon. Fri. 14.00.
Barons	17c	Macleod	Calgary / Lethbridge		Dy. tr. 512 C.P.R. / Dy. tr. 511 C.P.R.
Barrhead	21	Edmonton	Edmonton	~~Clyde~~	Dusseldorf ~~Tue.~~ Sat. 8.00.
Barrhill	17c	Med. Hat	Lethbridge / Calgary	Carmangay	M. W. F. 8.00.
Barnwell	17	Med. Hat	M. H. & N. (1)		Dy. tr. 511
Bartlettville	21	Strathcona	Edmonton		Mon. Fri. tr. ~~35~~ C.N.R.
Bashaw	~~17c~~	Red Deer	Calgary / Edmonton / Camrose		Dy. tr. 11 G.T.P. / Dy. Tr. 12 G.T.P.
*Bassano	17	Med. Hat	M. J. & C.		Dy. trs. 1, 2, 3, 4.
Bathgate	14	Victoria	N. B. & E.	Mundare	Fri. 8.30.
Battenburg	21	Edmonton	Edmonton	New Lunnon	~~Tue.~~ Sat. 9.00.
Battlebend	24	Red Deer	S. & H. / H. & W.	Hardisty	Tue. Sat. 13.30.
Battle Lake	~~20~~ 24	Strathcona	Wetaskiwin		T. T. S. 8.00.
Battle Ridge	24	Red Deer	S. & H.	Amisk	Mon. Fri. 8.30.
Battleview	14	Strathcona	Vermilion		Tue. Fri. 9.00.
Bawlf	14c	~~Strathcona~~	H. & W.		Dy. trs. 527, 528.
Bearberry	20	Red Deer	C. & E.	Olds	Sundre, Fri. 16.00.
Bear Lake	21	Edmonton	Edmonton	Peace R. ~~Cross.~~	~~Wed. Sat.~~ 8.00.
Beaumont	20	Strathcona	C. & E.	Leduc	T. T. S. 10.00.
Beauvallon	14	Victoria	Vegreville	Duvernay	Fri. 13.30.
Beaver Crossing	14	Victoria	Vegreville	Durningville	Wed. ~~7.00~~.

OFFICE	KEY No.	COUNTY	DISTRIBUTION		

Office	Key No.	County	Distribution		
Beaver Hills...	14	Victoria...	Ft. Sask n.	.	T. T. S. 9.[illegible]0.
Beaver Lake..	14	Victoria	N. B. & E.	Mundare.	Fri. 8.30.
Beaver Lodge.	21	Edmonton..	Edmonton..	Grande Prairie.	Wed. Sun. 7.00
Beaver Mines..	18	Macleod...	M. H. & N	Pincher Creek..	M. W Sat. 9.00.
Beazer...	18a	Med. Hat..	Lethbridge..	Cardston.	Tue. Thu. Sat 6.00.
Beddington.	17	Calgary	C. & E. (1)	.	Dy. trs. 523, 524
Beiseker....	17c	Calgary...	Calgary..	.	[illegible]
Bellevue.	18	Macleod...	M. H. & N.	.	Dy. trs. 51[illegible], 51[illegible].
Bellcamp.	14	Vi[illegible]	N B. & E.	Kitscoi	Marwayne M. Th. 14.00.
Bellis...	14	Victoria...	N B. & E ..	Lamont.	Edwand, Sat. 10.30.
Bellshill.	14c	Strathcona	H. & W..	Sedgewick	Merna Wed. Sat. 14.00.
Belvedere..	21	Edmonton..	Edmonton.	Busby	Tue. Fri. [illegible].00.
Bentley..	20	Red Deer..	Lacombe..	.	Dy. 8.00.
Benton Station....	15f	Med. Hat.	S. & C...	..	Dy. tr.
Bergen..	20	Red Deer...	C. & E...	Didsbury.	Elkton, Tue. Sat. 13.60.
Berry Creek.....	15f	Med Hat...	S. & C..	Stanmore.	M. W F. 8.30.
Berrymoor...	30a	Edmonton..	Gainford....	Tomahawk	Tue. 12.30.
Beverly ..	21	Edmonton.....	Edmonton.	..	Dy. ~~10.00~~
Beynon...	15f	Med. Hat..	S. & C..	...	Dy. tr. ~~21~~
Bezanson.....	21	Edmonton..	Edmonton.	Grande Prairie.	Sun. 7.00.
Bickerdike...	30a	Edmonton.....	Ed. & P. G.	.	Mon. tr. [illegible] Tue. tr. 91. Wed. Sat. tr. [illegible] Mon. Thur. tr [illegible]
Big Prairie...	17	Calgary...	C. & E. [illegible]	Carstair	Tue., Fri., 10.30.
Big Spring..	15f	Med. Hat...	S. & C...	Chinook...	Wed. 8.00.
Big Stone...	15f	Med. Hat..	S. & C...	Chinook	Mon. Thur [illegible]
Big Valley...	26	Red Deer......	Mun. & Cam...	...	M.W.F. tr. 35. T. T. S. tr. 36.
Bingley.....	20	Red Deer......	Red Deer...	Leslieville..	Sat. ~~16.00~~.
Bingville..	17	Med. Hat...	Suffield St n....	..	Fri. 7.00.
Birdsholm.......	18a	Med. Hat....	Lethbridge.....	~~Warner~~..	~~Gudrun, Tue. Fri. 13.00~~
Bismark...	20	Red Deer.....	C. & E........	Ponoka...	Tue. Fri. 7.00.

OFFIC.	I.. . No.	.NTY	DIS RIB TION	

OFFICE	KEY No.	COUNTY	DISTRIBUTION		
Bittern Lake. . . .	14c	Strathcona. .	H. & W. .		[illegible] 47,
Black Diamond. . .	19	Macleod. .	Mac. & Cal. Calgary. .	[illegible]	T. T. 14.00.
Blackfalds	20	Red Deer.	C. & E.		Dy. [illegible] 524, 525, 526.
Blackfoot. .	14	Victoria	N. B. & E.		Dy. [illegible] Mon. tr. 2.
Blackie. . .	17c	Macleod. . .	Calgary . Lethbridg		Dy tr. 512 C.P.R. Dy tr. 511 C.P.R.
Black Spring Ridge.	17c	Med. Hat.	Lethbridge Calgary	Carm[illegible]	M. W. F. [illegible].00.
Black Tail.	19	Macleod	Mac. & Cal.	[illegible]	Wed. 14.00.
Blairmore. . .	18	Macleod.	M. H. & N.		Dy. tr [illegible]
Blakesville. .	18a	Med. Hat.	Lethbri[illegible]	[illegible]	W[illegible] 12.[illegible]0
Blind Creek. .	17c	Macleod.	Calgar[illegible] Lethbri[illegible]	Bl[illegible]	T. T. [illegible].00.
Blondheim. . . .	20	Strathcona	C. & E.	Led[illegible]	Co[illegible] Creek [illegible]t. 16.30.
Bluesk[illegible]	21	Edmonton.	Edmonton.	Pon[illegible]	Wed. Sat. 8.00.
Bluff Centre . .	20	Red Deer. . .	C. & E	Ponok[illegible]	Tue. Fri. 7.00.
Boian	14	Victoria. . .	Vegreville. .	Warwi[illegible]	[illegible] Lake, [illegible] 15.00.
Bon Accord. . .	21	Edmonton.	Edmonton. .	[illegible]	[illegible]
Bon [illegible]. . .	14c	Strathcona. .	H. & W.	m[illegible]	Tue. Fr[illegible].00.
Bonnie Glen. . .	20	Strathcona.	C. & E. . .	Mill[illegible]	[illegible] 14.00
Bonnyville. .	14	Victoria	Vegreville.	St. Paul de Metis	Tue [illegible]t. 7.00.
Bordenave.	14	Victoria. . . .	Vegreville. . . .	St. Paul de Metis	T. T. S. 1[illegible].00.
Borradaile.	14	Victoria	N. B. & E.		[illegible] tr. [illegible]
Borszczow. . . .	14	Victoria .	Vegreville. .		[illegible] tr. 157 C. N. R.
Botha.	14d	Red Deer .	C. & E.		Dy tr. 5[illegible]9, 530.
Bottrell.	17	Calgary. . .	C. & V. (No. 1)	Cochrane	Wed. Sat. 7.00.
Boundary Creek. .	18a	Med. Hat. . .	Lethbridge	[illegible]ardston,	Fri. 13.45.
Bouvier. . .	21	Victoria. . .	Edmonton.	Athabaska.	Tue. 7.00
Bowden.	20	Red Deer. . .	C. & E. . .		Dy. trs. 523, 524, 525, 526.
Bowell.	17	Med. Hat. . .	M. J. & C.		Dy trs. 3, 4.

OFFIC	KEY No.	CO'' TY	DISTRIBUTION		

OFFICE	KEY No.	COUNTY	DISTRIBUTION		
Bow Island	17	Med. Hat	M. H. & N. (1)		Dy.* trs [illegible]13, 514. Dy. trs. 511 [illegible]12.
Bowmanton	17	Med. Hat	~~M. J. & C.~~	~~Pashley~~	Mon. [illegible].00
Bow Valley	19	Macleod	Mac. & Cal. Calgary	Stavely	Sat. 13.00.
Box Springs	17	Med. Hat	M. J. & C.	Redcliff	Fri. 13.00.
Boyne Lake	14	Victoria	Vegreville	Duvernay	~~Tue.~~ 8.00.
Bragg Creek	17c	Calgary	Calgary	Jumping Pound	Sat. 14.00
Brant	17c	Macleod	Calgary. Lethbridge		Dy tr. 51[illegible] C.P.R. Dy tr [illegible]11 C. R
Br[illegible]wford	17[illegible]	Med Hat	~~M. J. & C.~~	[illegible]ssano.	M. W. F. [illegible]
Breda	17c	Red Deer	Calgary. Edmonton	[illegible]	[illegible] 1[illegible]30.
Bredin	21	Edmonton	Edmonton	Grande Prairie	Wed. [illegible]00
Bremner	~~22b~~	Edmonton	~~W. & E.~~		Dy [illegible]
Bridstow	14	Victoria	C. B. & E.	Islay	Sat. 10.30.
Bright Bank	30	Edmonton	Ed. & P. G. (1	[illegible] Pla[illegible]	Mon [illegible]
Brightview	24	Strathcona	Wetaskiwin.		T. T. [illegible]00.
Brightwood	30a	Edmonton	[illegible] P. G	[illegible]	[illegible]
Britain	14d	Red Deer	C. & L.	Falkirk	Tue. Fri. [illegible].00.
Brocket	18	Macleod	M. H. & N.		Dy [illegible] ~~514~~
Brooksley	20	Red Deer	Lacombe.		Tue [illegible]0.
Brooks Station	17	Med. Hat	M. J. & C.		Dy. [illegible]
Brosseau	14	Victoria	Vegreville.		Dy. [illegible]00.
Brownfield	14d	Red Deer	Coronation		[illegible]
Bruce	22b	Strathcona	[illegible] & E.		[illegible]
Bruederheim	14	Victoria	C. B. & E		Dy [illegible]
Brutus	17	Med. Hat	[illegible]field [illegible]		Fri. 7.[illegible]
Buckhorn	20	Red Deer	[illegible] & E.	Ponoka.	Tue. [illegible] 7.00.
Buffalo View	24	Strathcona	[illegible] & H.	Hughender	[illegible] 1[illegible]30.
Buford	20	Strathcona	[illegible] & E.	Leduc.	[illegible] 13.00.
Bulwark	14d	Red Deer	C. & L.	Fede[illegible]	We[illegible] [illegible]00.
Burdett	17	Med. Hat	M.H. & N. (1		Dy. [illegible] 11, 512. Sun. t[illegible] ~~513, 514~~.

OFFICE	KEY No.	COUNTY	DISTRIBUTION

Office	Key No.	County	Distribution		
Burfield.	15f	Med. Hat. . . .	S. & C	Hanna. .	Mon. Thur. 8.00
Burmis.	18	Macleod. . . .	M. H. & N	. . . .	Dy. trs. ~~513~~, [illegible]
Burnt Lake. . . 6 . .	20	Red Deer. . . .	Red Deer. . . .	. . . . . .	T. T. S. 13.30.
Burtonsville.	30a	Edmonton. . . .	Ed. & P. G.	Gainford. .	~~Mon~~. Fri. 7.00.
7 Busby.	21	Edmonton.	Edmonton.	.	Mon. Thur. tr. 1 E. D. & B. C.
Bushland.	14	Victoria. .	N. B. & F	Mannville.	Naughton Glen. 16.00

Office	Key No.	County	Distribution		
	[illegible]	[illegible]	[illegible]	[illegible]	[illegible] Sat. 9.30
.18 Cadomin	[illegible]	[illegible]	Edson	[illegible]	Alta Coal Br. [illegible]
			[illegible]	[illegible]	[illegible]
	[illegible]	[illegible]	[illegible]	[illegible]	[illegible] Thur. 11.30

Office	Key No.	County	Distribution		
Cadogan...	24	Red Deer..	S. & H.		Dy. tr. 51, 52.
Cairns...	24	Red Deer..	S. & H. ..		Dy. tr. 52.
Calais..	21	Edmonton.	Edmonton.	Grande Prairie.	Tu. 7.00
Caldbeck.	17	Calgary...	C. & V. (1)	Cochrane	Sat. 13.00.
Caldwell.	18a	Med. Hat	Lethbridge..	Cardston.	Tu. Thu. 6.00.
Calendula. ...	15f	Med. Hat.	S. & C..	Alsask ..	Sa 8.30.
*Calgary.		Calgary....			
Calmar..	20	Strathcona..	C. & E.	Leduc	Wed. Sat. 10.00
Campbell Hill..	29	Red Deer. ..	Corona jn.	Veteran..	Endsleigh, Sat 11.15
Campbell Lake...	14	Victoria.	Vermilion		Tue. 8.00.
Campsie....	21	Edmonton..	Edmonton..	Busby	Mos ide Wed. Sat. 12.00
Camrose..	14c	Strathcona..	C. & E.. H. & W... S. & H.... Mun. & Cam. Edmonton. Calgary .. Wetaskiwin..		Dy. [illegible], C. P. R. Dy. trs. 527, 528. Dy. ex. Mon. tr. 51. T. T. S. [illegible] Dy. tr. 52, C.P.R. Dy. tr. 12, G. T. P. Dy via tr. 11, G. T. P. Dy. via tr. 52, C. P. R.
Canmore...	17	Calgary... ..	C. & V. (No. 1)		Dy.* trs. 3, 4.
Cannell...	21	Edmonton...	Edmonton..		M. W. F. tr. 100, C.N.R. T. T. S. tr. 169, C.N.R.
Cappon...	15f	Med. Hat...	S. & C..	Excel.	Mon. Thu. 8.00.
Carbon..	17c	Med. Hat...	Calgary..	Grainger St'n	Dy. 13.45
Cardiff..	21	Edmonton..	Edmonton...	Morinville.	T. T. S. 15.15. M. W F. 10.45.
*Cardston...	18a	Med. Hat...	Lethbridge...	.....	Dy. tr. 538, C. P. R.
Carloss....	20	Red Deer..	Red Deer....	Leslieville	Thur. 12.30.
Carmangay.	17c	Macleod.....	Lethbridge.. Calgary....		Dy. tr. 511, C. P. R. Dy tr. 512, C. P. R.
Carnforth....	19	Macleod.....	Mac. & Cal. Calgary..	Granum..	Tue. Fri. 15.00.
Caroline...	20	Red Deer.....	Red Deer.	Rocky Mt. House.	T. T. S. 7.00.
Carrot Creek..	30a	Edmonton..	Ed. & P. G.	Peers	Tue. Fri. 8.00.
Carseland...	17	Macleod	M. J. & C.		Dy. tr. ..
Carstairs...	17	Calgary...	C. & E. (1).		Dy. trs. 523, 524, 525, 526.

OFFICE	KEY No.	COUNTY	DISTRIBUTION

OFFICE	KEY No.	COUNTY	DISTRIBUTION		
Carvel Station..	30	Edmonton..	Ed. & P. G. (1).		T. T. S. tr. 3.
Casavant...	21	Edmonton...	Edmonton..	Legal..	Tue. Sat. 10.45
Castor....	14d	Red Deer...	C. & L.		Dy. trs. 529, 530.
Caseleyville...	14d	Red Deer..	Coronation..		M.W.F. 18.30.
Catchem...	17	Med. Hat.	~~M. H. & N. (1)~~	Seven Persons.	(Manyberries) Wed. 13.00.
Cayley..	19	Macleod..	Mac. & Cal.. ~~Calgary~~..		Dy. trs. 537-540. Dy. tr. 539, C. P. R.
Cereal...	15f	Med. Hat.	S. & C..		Dy. trs 23, 24.
Cessford	17	Med. Hat..	Bassano Empress	[illegible]ville.	[illegible]
Chailey...	14	Victoria.	N. B. & [illegible]	Mannville	[illegible] 7.00.
Champion..	17c	Macleod..	Lethbridge. Calgary.		Dy. tr. 511, C. P. R. Dy. tr. 512, C. P. R.
Chateau Lake Louise (s)...	17	Calgary..	C. & V. (1)..		Dy. [illegible]
Chauvin..	22a	Strathcona..	Riv. & Wain..		Dy. [illegible] 1, 2.
Cheadle.	17	Calgary...	M. J. & C.		Dy. trs. 3, 4.
Cherhill.	21.	Edmonton..	Edmonton..		Wed. [illegible] C.N.R.
Chesterwold..	20	~~Strathcona~~.	C. & E	Ponoka..	Tue. Fri. 14.00.
Chigwell..	14d	Red Deer..	C. & L.		Dy. trs. 529, 530.
Chilmark..	15f	Med. Hat..	S. & C..	[illegible]ook	Wed. 8.00.
Chin..	17	Med. Hat..	M. H. & N. (1	..	Dy. tr. 511.
Chinook...	15f	Med. Hat...	S. & C..		Dy. [illegible], 24.
Chipman.	14	Victoria.	N. B. & E.		Dy. * trs. 1, 2.
Claresholm...	19	Macleod..	Mac. & Cal.. ~~Calgary~~..... M. H. & N.		[illegible] 537, 540. Dy. [illegible]38, C.P.R. Dy. [illegible]9.
Clarinda..	18a	Med. Hat..	Lethbridge..	Coutts..	[illegible] Sat. [illegible].00.
Clark Manor..	22b	Strathcona...	W. & E...	Irma..	Wed. Sat. 16.30.
Clemens...	15f	Med. Hat...	S. & C......	Cereal..	Mon. Thu. ~~8.00.~~
Clive......	14d	Strathcona...	C. & L.		Dy. trs. 529, 530.
Clodford...	14	~~Victoria~~.	Fort Sask'n.....	Myrtle Creek.	~~Wed. 9.30.~~
Clover Bar...	~~22b~~	Edmonton..	~~W. & E.~~		Dy. trs. 1, 2.
Cluny Station...	17	Med. Hat.....	M. J. & C.		Dy. tr. 3, 4.
Clyde........	21	Edmonton..	Edmonton..		M. W. F. tr. 105, C. N. R.

OFFICE	KEY No	COUNTY	DISTRIBUTION

Office	Key No.	County	Distribution		
Clymont.	30	Edmonton.	Ed. & P. C	Spruce Grove	Tue. Fri. 15.00
Clystie..	15f	Med. Hat...	[illegible] & C..	Mecheche.	Wed. 12.1[illegible]
Coaldale..	17	Med. Hat...	M. H. & N. (1		Dy tr [illegible] 511. 51
Coalhurst...	[illegible]	Med. Hat	M. H. [illegible]		[illegible]
Coalspur. ...	30a	Edmonton.	[illegible]		W[illegible] Fri. [illegible] Alt[illegible] Br[illegible] T. P.
Cochrane...	17	Calgary	C. & V. (No. 1		Dy tr [illegible]
Cold Lake.	14	Victoria	Vegreville	B[illegible] Cross	Thur 12 [illegible]0.
Coleman....	18	Macleod...	M. H. & N		Dy tr [illegible] 14
Coleridge.	17	Med. Hat.	M. J. & C		Dy
Colinton..	21	Edmonton..	Edmonton		M. W F [illegible] N.P
Collholme...	15.	Med. Hat...	[illegible] &	[illegible]k..	Mon. Thur. [illegible]
Columbine.	14	Victoria	[illegible]	[illegible]	Hendon [illegible] 1[illegible].
Commerce..	18	Med. Hat...	M. H. [illegible]		Dy
Compeer..	29	Red Deer.	[illegible] E[illegible] Rob[illegible]		[illegible] W. [illegible] P.R. T. T. [illegible] P.R.
Comrey...	17	Med. Hat..	M. H. & N. (1)	Seven Persons	Manyb[illegible] W [illegible]
Condor.....	20	Red Deer	Red Deer.		M. W [illegible] P.R.
Conjuring Creek.	20	Strathcona.	[illegible] & E.	[illegible]educ	[illegible]d. 10.[illegible]
Connolly...	14	Victoria	Vermilion.		Tue. [illegible].
Connor Creek.	21	Edmonton..	[illegible]lmo	[illegible]	[illegible] 17.00
Connorsville...	[illegible]	Med. Hat.	[illegible]	[illegible]awford.	[illegible] Thur.
Consort...	29	Red Deer..	[illegible] K [illegible]		[illegible] P.R.
Cooking Lake...	22b	Strathcona..	W. & E...	[illegible]	[illegible]
Cookville.	14	Victoria.			[illegible]
Coppice Hill.	[illegible]	Victoria.		[illegible]dro	[illegible]
Cork...	14	Victoria	[illegible] B[illegible] E.	[illegible]	[illegible] Lake [illegible] 1.00.
Cornucopia.	14a	Red Deer...	[illegible]	[illegible]	Tue. T[illegible] 14.00
Coronation....	14d	Red Deer	[illegible] Robert.		[illegible] T. [illegible]
Cosmo...	21	Edmonton..	Edmonton	[illegible]	
Cotterview	14	Victoria.	N. B. & E.	Mannvill.	[illegible] 14.00

Office	Key No.	County	Distribution		

OFFICE	KEY No.	COUNTY	DISTRIBUTION		
Cousins....	24	Red Deer..	S. & H.	Cadogan...	Sat. 13.00.
*Coutts....	18a	Med. Hat..	Lethbridge..		Dy. tr. 564, C.P.R.
Cowley....	18	Macleod..	M. H. & N...	. . .	Dy.*trs. 513, 514.
Coyote Valley.....	14	Victoria.	Vermilion.	.	8.00.
Craigmillar........	24	Red Deer..	S. & H.	Czar.	Wed. 9.00.
Craig Murray..	15f	Med. Hat...	S. & C..	Cereal.	Thu. 14.00.
Craigmyle.........	15f	Red Deer..	S. & C.	. . . .	Dy. tr. 24. Dy. ex. Mon. 22
Cravath Corners....	17	Med. Hat...	Bassano. Empress	Steveville.	Tue. Fri. 13.00.
Cremona..	17	Calgary.....	C. & E. (1).	Carstairs.	Tue. Fri. 10.30.
Crippsdale.....	14	Edmonton.	Fort Sask'n.	Egremont.	Sat. 8.00
Crossfield. ..	17	Calgary...	C. & E. (No. 1)	..	Dy. trs 523, 524, 525, 526.
Crowfoot.......	17	Med. Hat....	M. J. & C.	.	Tue. Fri. tr. 3.
Culham.........	17c	Red Deer...	Calgary. Edmonton.	Delburne	Mon. Fri. 16.00.
Cummings....	14	Strathcona..	Vermilion......	.	Tue. Fri. 9.00.
Curlew..	17c	Red Deer.	Calgary Edmonton.	Trochu	Tue. Fri. 7.00.
Czar....	24	Red Deer....	S. & H.		Dy. 1, 52.

OFFICE	KEY No.	COUNTY	DISTRIBUTION

OFFICE	KEY No.	COUNTY	DISTRIBUTION		
Dalemead..	17	Macleod	M. J. & C		[illegible]y tr [illegible]
Dalmuir...	14	Victoria.	Fort S[illegible]k'n	Myrtle C[illegible]	[illegible]
Dalro[illegible]...	17c	Calgary..	Calgary		[illegible] C.P.[illegible]
Dauntless....	17	Med. Hat.	M. H. & [illegible]		[illegible] 511. [illegible] T. S. [illegible]12.
Davisburg.	19	Macleod..	Ma[illegible] & Cal.. Calgary	De Win[illegible]	[illegible] 9.1
Daysland...	14c	~~Strathcona~~..	H. & W		[illegible] 27,
Deering ..	17	Med Hat.	~~Suffield Sta~~	[illegible]lav	[illegible] Sa[illegible] 1[illegible]00
Deer Mound..	21 ~~22b~~	Strathcona..	W. & [illegible]	[illegible]	[illegible] 12[illegible]0.
Del[illegible]our.	17[illegible]	Calgary	Calgar[illegible]		[illegible] T. S. [illegible]11, [illegible] T.P.
Delano..	1[illegible]	Med. Hat...	~~Bassa.~~ Empre[illegible]	[illegible]	[illegible] 14.0[illegible]
Del Bonita..	18a	Med Hat	Lethbri[illegible]	[illegible]	[illegible]00.
Delburne	17c	Red Deer	[illegible]algar[illegible] Edmonton		[illegible] 11 [illegible] 12 [illegible]
Del[illegible]..	1[illegible]	Red Dee[illegible]	[illegible] & C		[illegible] tr. 24. D[illegible] ex M.
Delph..	14	V[illegible]ria.	[illegible] B. & E	[illegible]am	[illegible]00.
Denisville...	1[illegible]	V[illegible]	[illegible]gr[illegible]ville	Pa[illegible] Me[illegible]	T. T. [illegible] 14[illegible]
Desjarlais.	1[illegible]	Victo[illegible]	[illegible] B. &	[illegible]	[illegible]
De Kota..	14	V[illegible]	V[illegible]mil[illegible]n.	[illegible]	[illegible]15
Deville..	22b	[illegible]athcona	[illegible] & E..		Mon. W[illegible]d [illegible]
Dewberry.....	14	Victoria	[illegible].. B. [illegible]	[illegible]	[illegible]
De Winton.....	19	Macleod.	Mac. & Ca[illegible] Calgary.		[illegible]0 [illegible]
Diamond City.	~~18~~	~~Med. Hat~~...	[illegible] & [illegible]		
Dick[illegible]n.	20	Red Deer,	[illegible] & E	[illegible]	[illegible]
Didsbury...	20	~~Red Deer~~..	[illegible] &		[illegible] 524 525 [illegible]52
Diligence...	21	Edmonton..	[illegible]ton..	[illegible]	[illegible] 13.0
Dina....	14	Strathcona..	[illegible] & E..	[illegible]	Mon [illegible] 7[illegible]0.
Dinant..	21	Strathcona..	Edmont[illegible]n..		M. V [illegible] T.[illegible]
Dinton...	17c	Macleod...	Calgary.. Lethbridge.	Blackie	[illegible]T.[illegible]00

OFFICE	KEY No	COUNTY	DISTRIBUTION		

Office	Key No.	County	Distribution		
Dnipro..	20	Strathcona.....	C. & E..	Leduc..	Thorsby, Mon. 14.00.
Dodds...	14	Strathcona...	Vegreville..... Camrose..		T.T.S. tr. 157, C.N.R. M. W F. tr. 158, C.N.R.
Dog Pound.	17	Calgary.......	C. & V. (No. 1)	Cochrane.	Wed. Sat. 7.00.
Doley..	22a	Strathcona...	Riv. & Wain.	Edgerton St'n.	Tue. Fri. 14.30.
Donalda....	26	Red Deer......	Mun. & Cam..		M.W.F. tr. 35, T.T.S. tr. 36.
Donatville..	21	Vi[illegible]	Edmonton	Athabaska	Tue. 8.00.
Dorenlee....	21	Red [illegible]er..	Edmonton.. Camrose..		Dy tr. 1[illegible] G.T.P.
Dorothy..	15f	Med. Hat...	[illegible]. & C..	[illegible]	Mon. 8.[illegible]0, Thur. 9.00.
Dovercourt.	20	Red Deer.	Red Deer	Rocky Mt. House.	T. T. [illegible] 7.00.
Dowling Lake..	15f	Red Deer.	[illegible]. &	Craigmyle.	Tue. Fri. 8.00.
Downing.....	14	Victoria.	N. B. & E.	Lamont..	Mon. Th. 7.00.
Drumheller.	15f	Med. Hat...	S. & C. .		Dy. Dy ex Mon. tr. 23
Dry Fork	18	Macleod..	M. H. & N...	Pincher Creek.	Tue. Fri. 8.00.
Duagh...	21	Edmonton..	Edmonton..		M. W F. 6.30.
Duchess.	17	Med. Hat.	Bassano... Empress		Mon. Thur. tr. 670, C.P.R. Tue. Fri. tr. 671, C.P.R.
Duffield.	30	Edmonton..	Ed. . P. C. 1,		[illegible] tr. 91. Mon. Thur. [illegible] 1. T. T. S. tr [illegible] Sat.[illegible]
Duhamel.	21	Strathcona...	Edmonton.. Camrose.		Dy tr. 1[illegible], G.T.P.
Dunn........	22a	Strathcona...	Riv. & Wain..		Dy. tr. 1.
Dunstable.	21	Edmonton..	Edmonton.	Busby	Tue. Fri. [illegible].
Dunvegan.	21	Edmonton..	Edmonton	[illegible] R. [illegible]	Wed. [illegible]
Durlingville...	14	Victoria.	Vegreville...	St. Paul de Metis	Tue. Sat. 7.00.
Dusseldorf...	21	Edmonton.	Edmonton.	Clyde	Hazel Bluff, Mon. Fri. 18.00.
Duvernay........	14	Victoria.	Vegreville...		Dy. 8.00.

OFFICE	KEY No.	COUNTY	DISTRIBUTION	

OFFICE	KEY No.	COUNTY	DISTRIBUTION		
Eagle Butte......	17	Med. Hat....	Medi. ..e Hat		Tue. Fri. 7.45
Eagle Hill...	20	Red Deer.	C. & E.	Old.	Tue Fri 8.00.
Earlie..	14	Strathcona..	S. B. & I	K.	Tue Fri 8.00.
Earlstone....	17	Med. Hat...	Bassano.. Richdale		M.W. 8.00
Earlville....	14d	Red Deer.	C. & L.	Te	Tue Fri 10.00.
Eastburg.	21	Edmonton..	Edmonton..	Clyde	Hazel Bluff, ...on Fri. 1S-1
Eastgate....	14	Edmonton..	Ft. Sask'n.		Tue. Fri ...
East Lorraine.	14d	Red Deer	Coronation.	Brownfield.	Tue ..t. 10.30.
Eastway....	17c	Macleod...	Calgary... Lethbridge.	Vulcan..	Tue Sat. 8.00.
Echohill	21	Edmonton..	Edmonton	Bu. by	Tue 10.00.
Eckville...	20	Red Deer...	Red Deer..		M. W. F. tr. 618, C.P.R.
Edberg..	26	Strathcona....	Mun. & Cam.		M. W. F. .. 35. T. T. S. .. 36.
Edgerton Station...	22a	Strathcona...	Riv. & Wain...		Dy. trs. 1 2
*Edmonton.		Edmonton...	.....	....	
Edson...	30a	Edmonton...	Ed. & P. C		Mon. tr. 92. Mon. Thur. tr. 1. T. T. S. tr. 3. Wed. Sat. tr. 2. Tue. tr. 91.
Edwand....	14	Victoria...	H. & E..	Lamont..	Pakan, Tue. Fri. 14.00
Edwell.	20	Red Deer..	C. & E...	Penhold...	Wed. Sat. 7.45.
Egremont......	14	Edmonton..	Ft. Sask'n		Tue. Fri. 8.00.
Elbow River..	17c	Calgary......	Calgary........	.	Wed. Sat. .00.
Elcan.	17	Med. Hat.....	M. H. & N. (1).	Barnwell...	Dy. 8.45.
Eldorena....	14	Victoria...	Ft. Sask'n.		Tue. Fri. 8.00.
Elk Point.........	14	Victoria.......	Vermilion.....	...	Tue. Fri. 15.00.
Elkton..	20	Red Deer.....	C. & E......	Didsbury..	T. T. S. 7.00.
Elkwater.	17	Med. Hat.....	M. J. & C.	Irvine.........	Tue. Fri. 7.00.
Elnora...	17c	Red Deer....	Calgary.. ... Edmonton..		Dy. tr. 11, G.T.R. Dy. tr. 12, G.T.R.
Empress..	28	Med. Hat...	S. C. & Emp. Bassano.		M. W. F. tr. 669. Mon. Thur. tr. 670, C.P.R.
Enchant.	17	Med. Hat...	Suffield Sta.		Mon. Fri. tr. 665, C.P.R.

OFFICE	KEY No.	COUNTY	DISTRIBUTION		
Erin Lodge					

Office	Key No.	County	Distribution		
Endiang	14d	~~Red Deer~~	C. & L.	Halkirk	Tue. Fri. 14.00
Enilda	21	Edmonton	Edmonton		M. Th. tr. 1. E. D. & B. C.
Ensign	17c	Macleod	Calgary Lethbridge		Dy. tr. 512, C.P.R. Dy. tr. 511, C.P.R.
Ensleigh	29	Red Deer	Coronation Kerr Robert	Veteran	Mon. Fri. 11 30.
Entrance	30a	Edmonton	Ed. & P. G.		Mon. Thur. tr. 1. Tue. tr. 91.
Entwistle	30a	Edmonton	Ed. & P. G.		Mon. Thur. tr. 1. T. T. S. trs. 3, 4. Wed Sat tr. 2 Tue. tr. 91. Mon. tr. 92
Ernsted	30a	Edmonton	Ed. & P. G.		Mon. Thur. tr. 1 Wed. Sat. tr. 2. Tue. tr. 91.
Erskine	14d	Red Deer	C. & L.		Dy. trs. 529, 530.
Esther	22a	~~Red Deer~~	Riv. & Wain. Biggar	Loverna	Sat 13.00
Ethelwyn	14	Victoria	N. B. & E.	Islay	Dewberry Tue. Fri. 13 30
Etzikom	~~17~~	Med. Hat	~~M. H. & N.~~ (1)		Wed. Sat. 8.00.
Eunice	21	Edmonton	Edmonton		M. Thur. tr. 1, E. D. & B. C.
Eva	17	Med. Hat	M. J. & C	Irvine	Hilda, Sat. 13.00.
Evansburgh	30a	Edmonton	Ed. & P. G.	Entwistle	Dy. 9.35
Evarts	20	Red Deer	Red Deer		M. W. [illegible] 515, C.P.R.
Eveland	15f	Med. Hat	S. & C.	Stanmore	M. W. F. 17.00.
Evergreen	20	Red Deer	Red Deer	Pitcox	Mon. Fri. 17.00.
Ewelme	18	Macleod	Macleod	Wellsville	Wed. Sat. ~~13.00~~
Ewing	26	Red Deer	Mun. & Cam.	Big Valley	Mon. 14.00.
Excel	15f	Med. Hat	S. & C.		Dy. trs. 23, 24.
Excelsior	21	Edmonton	Edmonton	Namao	Mon. Fri. 12.00.
Exshaw	17	Calgary	C. & V. (No. 1)		Dy.* trs. 3-4.
Eye Hill	24	Red Deer	S. & H.	Provost	~~Sat. 7.00~~
Eyremore	17	~~Med. Hat~~	M. J. & C.	Brooks St'n	M. W. F. 7.00.

Office	Key No.	County	Distribution

OFFICE	KEY No.	COUNTY	DISTRIBUTION		
Fairacres....	15f	Med. Hat.....	S. & C.......	Oy n...	Fri. 8.00.
Fairydell......	21	Edmonton.....	Edmonton..	Tegal.	Mon. Fri. 13.30.
Faith......	18a	Med. Hat....	Lethbridge.	Warner.	~~Altorado~~ 00.
Falher.......... ..	21	Edmonton..	Edmonton...	~~McLennan.~~	Tue. ~~13.30~~.
Fallis............	30	Edmonton...	Ed. & P. G		T. T. S s. 3, 4.
Falun............	24	Strathcona....	Wetaskiwin.		T. T 3.00.
Favor......	~~17~~	~~Med. Hat~~..	Bassano. Richdale.		.00. .00.
Fawcett.	21	Edmonton..	Edmonton.		Mon. Thur. tr. 1, E. D. & B. C
Fawn Lake... ..	21	Edmonton..	Edmonton..	Bush	Tue. Fri. 15.15.
Federal...	14d	Red Deer......	C. & L.. ..		Dy. tr. 530.
Fedorah.. ..	21	Edmonton.	Edmonton..	~~New Lunnon~~..	Tue. Sat. 9.00.
Fenner..	15f.	Red Deer.	S. & C	Youngstown.	M W F. 00.
Ferguson Flats... .	14	Victoria..	Kitscoty..	Lea Park..	Mooswa Tue. Fri. 16.00.
Ferintosh... .. .	21	Strathcona..	Edmonton. Camrose..		Dy. r. 12, G.T.P.
Fern Creek... 24.	~~20~~	Strathcona...	C. & E.....	~~Millet~~...	Fisher Home, Fri. 8.00.
Ferrybank..	20	Red Deer......	C. & E..	Ponoka..	Tue. Fri. ~~14~~.00.
Ferry Point........	26	Red Deer... ..	Mun. & Cam.	Edberg.	Mon. Fri. 10.45.
Fertility..........	14d	~~Med. Hat~~.....	C. & L.. ..	Castor. .	Garden Plain, Mon. Fri. 13.00.
Fescue..........	14	Victoria. ..	N. B. & E.	Lamont.......	Wasel, Fri. 12.15.
Fishburn........ .	18	Macleod.....	M. H. & N..	Pincher Creek.	Tue. Fri. 8.00.
Fisher Home.... ..	20	Strathcona..	C. & E.	Millet...	Bonnie Glen, Mon. Thur. 12.00.
Flagstaff...	14c	Strathcona...	H. & W... ..	Sedgewick.	Tue. Fri. 8.00.
Flat Bush.........	21	Edmonton..	Edmonton..	. ...	M. Th. tr. 1, E. D. & B. C.
Flat Creek...... ..	21	Edmonton.....	Edmonton...	~~Colinton~~....	~~Sat. 8.00~~.
Flat Lake..... ..	14	Victoria... ..	Vegreville....	St.Paul de Metis	Tue. Sat. 7.00
Flaxland....	15f	Med. Hat.....	S & C.......	Stanmore....	Berry Creek—Baraca— Sat. 8.00.

62290—3½

Office	Key No.	County	Distribution		

Office	Key No.	County	Distribution		
Fleet	14d	Red Deer	C. & L.		Dy. tr. 530.
Florann	18a	Med. Hat	Lethbridge	Warner	Goddard, Tue. Fri. 15.00.
Flowerdale	15f	Med. Hat	S. & C.	Stanmore	Berry Creek, Mon. Fri. 14.00.
Forbesville	14	Victoria	N. B. & E.	Lloydminister	Union Lake [illegible] 17.00.
Forçina	15f	Med. Hat	S. & C.	Hanna	[illegible] 14.00.
Foreman	14d	Red Deer	C. & L.	Halkirk	Tue. Fri. 8.00.
Foremost	17	Med. Hat	M. H. & N. (1).	Burdett	Tue [illegible] 8.00.
Forestburg	14c	Strathcona	H. & W.	Daysland	Hastings Coulee, Tue. S. 10.00.
Forest Lawn	17c	Calgary	Calgary		Dy 8.00.
Fort Assiniboine	21	Edmonton	Edmonton	Clyde	Holmes Crossing, Mon. Wed. 11.00.
Fort Chipewyan	21	Victoria	Edmonton	Athabaska	9 times yearly
Fort Fitzgerald	21	Victoria	Edmonton	Athabaska	9 times yearly
Ft. McMurray	21	Victoria	Edmonton	Athabaska	5th of month. 9 times yearly
Fort Providence	21	Mack Terr.	Edmonton	Athabaska	Fort Smith 5 times yearly.
Fort Resolution	21	Mack Ter.	Edmonton	Athabaska	Fort Smith, 8 times yearly
Ft. Saskatchewan	14	Victoria	N. B. & E. / Edmonton		Dy. *trs. 1, 2. / Dy tr. 168, C.N.R.
Fort Simpson	21	N. W. T.	Edmonton	Athabaska	Fort Smith. 7 times yearly
Fort Smith	21	Mack Terr.	Edmonton	Athabaska	17 times per annum.
Ft. Vermilion	21	Edmonton	Edmonton	Peace R. Cros.	1st each mo. ex. Nov
Fountainstown	14d	Red Deer	C. & L.	Clive	Tue. Fri 14.00.
Fourways	17	Med. Hat	M. H. & N (1)	Seven Persons	Manyberries, Wed. Sat. 13.15.
Fox	17	Med. Hat	M. J. & C.	Walsh	Sat. 8.00.
*Frank	18	Macleod	M. H. & N.		Dy. *trs. 513, 514.
Frankburg	17c	Macleod	Calgary / Lethbridge	Blackie	Wed. Sat. 13.00.
Fraserton	15f	Med. Hat	S. & C.	Hanna	Mon. Thur. 8.00.

OFFICE	KEY No	COUNTY	DISTRIBUTION

Office	Key No.	County	Distribution		
7 Freeman River.....	21	Edmonton.....	Edmonton.....	~~Clyde~~......	Holmes Crossing Mon. Wed. 11.0
Freshfield........ 7	17e	Calgary.......	Calgary....		Wed. Sat. 14 30.
Fribourg...........	14	Victoria.......	Vegreville......	Duvernay.....	Beauvallon, Sat. 10.30.
Friedenstal.........	21	Edmonton.....	Edmonton...	Peace R. Cross	Wed. Sat. 8.00.
Frog Lake.........	14	Victoria....	V. R. & E....	Kitscoty...	Lea Park, Tue. Fri. 9.00.
Furman...........	19	Macleod....	Mac. & Cal.. Calgary...	Claresholm..	Sat. 10.30.

OFFICE	KEY No	COUNTY	DISTRIBUTION		

OFFICE	KEY No.	COUNTY	DISTRIBUTION		
Gadsby	14d	Red Deer	C. & L.		Dy. trs. 529, 530.
Gahern	18a	Med. Hat	Lethbridge	Warner	Altorado, Wed. S[illegible]. 10.30.
Gainford	30a	Edmonton	Ed. & P. G.		Mon. Thur. tr. 1. T. T. S. trs. 3, 4. Wed. Sat tr. 2. Tue. tr. 91. Mon. tr. 92.
Galahad	14c	Red Deer	H. & W.	Killam	[illegible]ue. Sat. 8.00.
Galarneauville	17	Med. Hat	~~Bassano~~ Richdale	~~Hutton~~	Tu[illegible] 1[illegible]30.
Garden Plain	14d	Red Deer	C. & L.	Castor	M. W. F. 7.00.
Garrington	20	Red Deer	C. & E.	Olds	Eagle Hill, Tue. Fri. 10.30.
Garth	20	Red Deer	Red Deer	Rocky Mt. House.	Sat. 11.30.
Gem	17	Med. Hat	[illegible]o.		[illegible] 00.
Ghost Pine Creek	17c	Red Deer	Calgary Edmonton	Three Hills	Tue. Thu. Sat. 8.00.
Gilbert	15f	Med. Hat	~~Stanmore~~	Berry Creek	~~Baraca,~~ Sat. 8.00.
Gilby	20	Red Deer	Red Deer.	Eckville	M. W. F. 16.30.
Gilpin	22b	Victoria	W. & E.	Viking	Tue. Fri. 8.00.
Gilt Edge	22a	Strathcona	W. & E. Riv. & Wain.	Wainwright	Sat. 8.00.
Gladys	19	Macleod	Mac. & Cal. Calgary	De Winton	T. T. S. 9.15.
Gleichen	17	~~Med. Hat~~	M. J. & C.		Dy.* trs. 3, 4, 1, [illegible]
Glen Banner	17	Med. Hat	~~M. H. & N. (1)~~	~~Seven Persons~~	Tu[illegible] ~~7.00~~
Glenbow	17	Calgary	C. & V. (No. 1)		Dy.* trs [illegible]
Glendon	14	Victoria	Vegreville	St. Paul de Metis.	[illegible], Mon. Fri. ~~11.15~~.
Glenevis	21b	Edmonton	Edmonton		Wed. Sat. tr. ~~195~~, C.N.R.
Glenford	21	Edmonton	Edmonton	Busby	Sion, Tue. 15.15.
Glengarden 21	~~22b~~	Strathcona	~~W. & E.~~	Ardrossan	Tue. Sat. 10.15.
Glenglow 6	21	Victoria	Edmonton	(Athabaska)	Sat. 13.30.
Glenhewitt	20	Red Deer	Lacombe	Lochinvar	Wed. Sat. 13.30.
Gleniffer	20	Red Deer	C. & E.	Innisfail.	Tue. 13.30.
Glenister	21	Edmonton	Edmonton	Peavine	Thur. 13.30.

OFFICE	KEY No	COUNTY	DISTRIBUTION		

Office	Key No.	County	Distribution		
Glen Leslie	21	Edmonton	Edmonton	Gr. Prairie	~~Sun. 7.00.~~
Glenreagh	21	Edmonton	Edmonton	Clyde	Dusseldorf, Tue. Sat. 8.00.
Glenshaw	21	Edmonton	Edmonton	Flat Creek	Sat. 13.30.
Glenview	17c	Macleod	Calgary / Lethbridge	Blackie	T.T.S. 8.00.
Glenwoodville	18a	Macleod	Lethbridge	Cardston	Mon. Fri. 7.30.
Glevennah	28	Med. Hat	Empress		Tue. Sat. 13.00.
Glidehurst	20	Strathcona	C. & E.	Leduc	Fri. 12.30.
Goddard	18a	Med. Hat	Lethbridge	Warner	Tue. Fri. 7.00.
Golden Hill	15f	Med. Hat	S. & C.	Hanna	Tue. Sat. 11.00.
Golden Spike	30	Edmonton	Ed. & P. G.	Stony Plain	Sat. 15.00.
Gold Spring	15f	Med. Hat	S. & C.	Excel	Thu. [illegible].00.
Good Hope	14	Victoria	Fort Sask'n.		T. T. S. 9.30.
Gopher Head	26	Red Deer	Mun. & Cam.	Big Valley	Tue. Sat. 14.00.
Grainger Station	17c	Med. Hat	Calgary		Dy. tr. 11, G.T.P.
Grainland	14c	Strathcona	H. & W.	Killam	Tue. Sat. 8.00.
Graminia	30	Edmonton	Ed. & P. G.	Spruce Grove	Tue. Fri. 15.00.
Grande Prairie	21	Edmonton	Edmonton	~~McLennan~~	~~Tue. Fri.~~ 12.00.
Grandin	14	Victoria	Vegreville	Duvernay	Tue. 8.00.
Granlea	17	Med. Hat	M. H. & N. (1)	Winnifred	~~Wed. Sat.~~ 8.00.
Granum	19	Macleod	Mac. & Cal.		Dy. trs. 537, 540.
			Calgary		Dy. tr. 538, C.P.R.
			M. H. & N.		Dy. tr. 539.
Grassy Lake	17	Med. Hat	M. H. & N. (1)		Dy.* trs. 513, 614 / Dy. trs. 511, 512.
Gratz	14	Victoria	Vermilion	Landonville	Wed. 8.00.
Graystones	14d	Red Deer	C. & L.	Castor	Garden Plain, Fri. 13.00.
Green Court	21	Edmonton	Edmonton	~~Sangudo~~	Wed. Sat. 14.00.
Green Glade	24	Strathcona	S. & H.	Hayter	Tue. Sat. 9.00.
Greenlawn	14	Victoria	N. B. & E.	Islay	Dewberry, Tue. Fri. 13.30
Greenshields	22a	Strathcona	Riv. & Wain.		Dy. trs. 1, 2.
Griffin Creek	21	Edmonton	Edmonton	Peace R. ~~Cross.~~	~~Wed. Sat.~~ 8.00.
Grosmont	21	Edmonton	Edmonton	Athabaska	Sat. 15.00.
Gros Ventre	17	Med. Hat	M. J. & C.	Coleridge	Tue. Fri. 13.00.

OFFICE	KEY No.	COUNTY	DISTRIBUTION		

Office	Key No.	County	Distribution		
Groton............	18a	Med. Hat......	Lethbridge...	Warner........	Coddard-Lucky Strike, Fri. 17.00.
Grouard...........	21	Edmonton....	Edmonton.....	....	M. Th. tr. 1. E. D. & B. C.
Gurneyville........	14	Victoria.......	Vegreville......	St. Paul de Metis.	Rife, Tue. Sat. [illegible].20.
Gunn..............	21	Edmonton.....	Edmonton. ...	Lac Ste. Anne..	Sat. 12.00.
Gwynne..........	14c	Strathcona.....	H. & W. .. .	. . ..	Dv. tr. 528.

OFFICE	KEY No.	COUNTY	DISTRIBUTION		

OFFICE	KEY No.	COUNTY	DISTRIBUTION		
Hacke	18a	Med. Hat	Lethbridge	Magrath	Fri. 8.00.
Haddock	30a	Edmonton	Ed. & P. G.	Peers	Fri. 8.00.
Hairy Hill	14	Victoria	Vegreville	Warwick	Tue. Fri. 10.30.
Halcourt	21	Edmonton	Edmonton	Grande Prairie	Beaver Lodge, 1st & 3rd Thur. 13.30.
Halfway Lake	21	Edmonton	Edmonton	Clyde	Mon. Fri. 13.30.
Halkirk	14d	Red Deer	C. & L.		Dy. trs. 529, 530.
Halley	14c	Strathcona	H. & W	Bittern Lake	M. W. F. 10.30.
Hamlin	14	Victoria	N. B. & E.	Lamont	Mon. Thu. 7.00.
Hand Hills	15f	Med. Hat	S. & C.	Craigmyle	Mon. 8.30, Thur. 9.00.
Hanna	15f	Med. Hat	S. & C.		Dy. ex. Mon. trs. 23, [illegible]
Hardieville	18a	Med. Hat	Lethbridge		Dy. 10.00.
Hardisty	24	Strathcona	H. & W. S. & H. Edmonton. C. & E. Wetaskiwin., Camrose		Dy. Ex. Mon. tr. 51. 52, C.P.R. Dy. [illegible] tr. 52, C.P.R.
Hargwen	30a	Edmonton	Ed. & P. G.		Mon. Thur. tr. 1. Wed. Sat. tr. 2. Tue. tr. 91. Sun. tr. 92.
Harmattan	20	Red Deer	C. & E.	Olds	Tue. Fri. 12.00.
Hartcliffe	17c	Red Deer	Calgary	Twining	Fri. 13.15.
Hartshorn	15f	Red Deer	S. & C.	Craigmyle	Tue. Fri. 8.00.
Hastings Coulee	14c	Strathcona	H. & W.	Daysland	M. W. F. 14.00.
Hathersage	21	Edmonton	Edmonton	Roydale	Thur. 7.00.
Haverigg	20	Strathcona	C. & E.	Ponoka	Nugent, Sat. 9.45.
Hawksdale	17	Med. Hat	Bassano Empress	Steveville	Wennington, Tue. Sat. 14.00.
Hay Creek	21	Edmonton	Edmonton		M. W. F. tr. 105, C.N.R.
Hay Lakes	21	Strathcona	Edmonton Camrose		Mon. Fri. tr. 35. C.N.R. Tue. Sat. tr. 36. C.N.R.
Hay River	21	Mack Terr	Athabaska	Fort Smith	8 times per annum.
Hayhurst	24	Strathcona	Wetaskiwin	Brightview	Tue. Sat 13.00.
Haynes	14d	Red Deer	C. & L.	Clive	Tue. Fri. 14.00.
Hayter	24	Red Deer	S. & H.		Dy. tr. 52.

OFFICE	KEY No.	COUNTY	DISTRIBUTION	

9.18 Hilli

Office	Key No.	County	Distribution		
Hazel Bluff..	21	Edmonton	Edmonton	~~Clyde~~	Westlock, Mon. Fri. 15.00
Hearnleigh	17c	Macleod	Lethbridge Calgary	Vulcan	[illegible] 8.00.
Heart Lake	15f	Red Deer	S. & C.	Craigmyle	Tue. Fri. 8.00.
Heath	22a	Strathcona	Riv. & Wain.		Dy. tr. 1, 2.
Heather Brae	14c	Strathcona	H. & W.	Ohaton	Tue. Fri. [illegible].30
Heath Creek	18	Macleod	M. H. & N.	Cowley	Fri. 13.30
Heathdale	15f	Med. Hat.	S. & C.	Chinook.	Mon. Thu. 7.30.
Heatherdown	21	Edmonton	Edmonton	Onow[illegible]	Wed. 11.[illegible]0
Heinsburg	14	Victoria	N. B. & E.	Kitscoty	Lea Park. Tue. Fri. 9.00.
Heisler	14c	Strathcona	H. & W.	Daysland	M. W. [illegible] 14.00.
Heldar	21	Edmonton	Edmonton	Roydale	Thur. 7.00.
Helmsdale	15f	Med. Hat	S. & C.	Excel	Sunnydale M. [illegible]00.
Hercules	20	Strathcona	C. & E.	[illegible]athcona.	M. W. [illegible] 8.00.
Hermit Lake	21	Edmonton	Edmonton.	Gr. Pr[illegible]	Wed. 7.00.
Herronton	17c	Macleod	Calgary Lethbridge	Blackie	T. T. S. 8.00.
Highland Park	21	Strathcona	Edmonton Camrose	New Norway	T. T. S. 8.00.
Highland Ranch	17c	Red Deer	Calgary Edmonton	Trochu	Sat. 13.30.
High Prairie	21	Edmonton	Edmonton		Mon. Th. tr. 1, E. D. & B. C.
High River	19	Macleod	Mac. & Cal. ~~Calgary~~ M. H. & N.		Dy trs. ~~537~~, 540. Dy. [illegible] 538 C.P.R. Dy. tr. 539.
High Vale	30	Edmonton	Ed. & P. G. (1)	Duffield	Mon. [illegible].00
Hilda	17	Med. Hat	M. J. & C.	Irvine	Tue. Fri. 8.00.
Hillcrest Mines	18	Macleod	M. H. & N.		Dy. tr. 513.
Hill End	20	Red Deer	C. & E.	Innisfail	Tue. Sat. 14.00.
Hillsdown	20	Red Deer	Red Deer		Wed. Sat. 8.00.
Hill Spring	18a	Macleod	Lethbridge	Cardston	Mon. Fri. ~~8.00~~.
Hindville	14	Victoria	N. B. & E.	Borradaile	Tue. Fri. 7.00.
Hinton	30a	Edmonton	Ed. & P. G.		Mon. ~~Thu.~~ tr. 1. Tue. Fri. tr. 2. Tue. tr. 91. Sun. tr. 92.

OFFICE	KEY No.	COUNTY	DISTRIBUTION		

OFFICE	KEY No.	COUNTY	DISTRIB[illegible]		
Hobbema..... ...	20	Strathcona....	C [illegible] E..		T. T. [illegible]
Holborn... .	30	Edmonton.....	[illegible] P. G	[illegible]ony Plain..	[illegible]on. F[illegible]
Holden.......	22b	Strathcona.....	W. & E..		Dy [illegible] 1,
Holmes Crossing....	21	Edmonton...	Edmonton.	[illegible]lyde.	Dusseldorf, Tue. S[illegible] 8.00.
Home Glen..	20	Strathcona..	[illegible] & E..	[illegible]onoka	[illegible]ue [illegible] 7.00.
Hope Valley... ...	22a	~~Strathcona~~..	Riv[illegible] & W[illegible] W[illegible] E.	[illegible]ight.	[illegible]
Hopkins....... .	14	Victoria.	V[illegible]		[illegible]
Horse Hills.. .	21	Edmonton	Edmo[illegible]n.		[illegible]
Horseshoe Canyon.	15f	Med. Hat	[illegible]	Dru[illegible]ller	[illegible].00
Horse Shoe Lake	20	Red Deer.	[illegible]	[illegible]ll.	[illegible] Velle Wed 1[illegible] 30
Hoselaw... .	14	Victoria	[illegible]gr[illegible]lle.	[illegible] Paul de M[illegible]	Rife, [illegible]
Howie..	17	Med. H	[illegible]o	[illegible]ville.	[illegible]3.00.
Hughenden.... .	24	Strathcona...	[illegible]d.		[illegible] trs 51,
Hunterville.. ..	20	Red Deer	[illegible]E	Dids[illegible]	[illegible]
Hussar.. .	17	Med. Hat	B[illegible]no.		
Hutton...... ...	17	~~Med. Hat~~	Ra[illegible] Ri[illegible]nd[illegible]		[illegible]
Huxley...	17c	Red Deer..	[illegible]ry [illegible]dmonton ..		[illegible] 11 T.P
Hythe..	21	Edmonton.. .	[illegible]on..	Beaver Lodge	

OFFICE	KEY No	COUNTY	DISTRIBUTION

OFFICE	KEY No.	COUNTY	DISTRIBUTION		
Iddesleigh	17	Med. Hat	Bassano		Mon. Thur. tr. 670, C.P.R.
			Empress		Tue. Fri. tr. 671, C.P.R.
Ingleton	14d	Red Deer	C. & L.	Castor	Tue. Sat. 7.15.
Inglis	17	Calgary	C. & V.	Cochrane	Fri. 8.30.
Innisfail	20	Red Deer	C. & E.		Dy. trs. 523, 526. Dy.* trs. 524, 525.
Innisfree	14	Victoria	N. B. & E.		Dy.* trs. 1, 2.
Iola	20	Strathcona	C. & E.	Ponoka	Bluff Centre, Wed. Sat. 8.00.
Irma	22a	Strathcona	W. & E. (1)		Dy. trs 1, 2.
Iron Springs	18a	Med. Hat	Lethbridge		M. W. F. Sat. 14.00.
Irricana	17c	Calgary	Calgary		Dy. tr. 11, G.T.P.
Irvine	17	Med. Hat	M. J. & C.		Dy.* trs. 3, 4, 1, 2.
Irwinville	14	Victoria	N. B. & E.	Islay	Tue. Fri. 8.15.
Islay	14	Victoria	N. B. & E.		Dy. trs. 1, 2.
Ispas	14	Victoria	N. B. & E.	Lamont	Desjarlais, Fri. 11.30.

OFFICE	KEY No.	COUNTY	DISTRIBUTION		

Office	Key No.	County	Distribution		
Jackville..........	17	Calgary........	C. & E. (No. 1[illegible]	Carstairs.	Tue Fri. 1[illegible]
Jarrow........	~~225~~	~~Strathcona~~.	W. & E. (1).	. . .	Dy. trs. 1, 2.
Jasper.....	30a	Edmonton...	Ed. & P G		Mon. Thur. tr Tue. Fri. tr. 2. Tue tr. 91. [illegible]un. tr. 92.
Jeffrey..........	21	Edmonton..	Edmonton.	Clyde ...	Mon. Fri. 13.30.
Jenner........	17	Med. Hat.....	Empress. Bassano.	. .	Tue Fri. tr 671, C.P.R. Mon. Thur tr. 670, C.P.R.
Jennings ...	17	Med. Hat.	Bassano. Empress	S[illegible]eveville	Pollockville Tu[illegible] [illegible]at ~~16.30~~.
Jethson.	15f	Med. Hat.	[illegible]. & C.	Stanmore	Berry Creek, Mon. Fri. 14.00.
Josephsburg.....	17	Med. Hat.	M. J. & C.	Irvine	Tue Fri. 7.00.
Jumping Pound. ...	17c	Calgary..	Calgary	. .	Wed. Sat. [illegible]
Junkins...........	30a	Edmonton..	[illegible] & P. G		T. T. [illegible] [illegible], 4

Office	Key No.	County	Distribution		

OFFICE	KEY No.	COUNTY	DISTRIBUTION		
Kahwin	14	Victoria	N. B. & E.	Lamont	Andrew, Fri. 7.30.
Kaleland	14	Victoria	Vegreville	Warwick	Hairy Hill, Wed. 8.00.
Kananaskis	17	Calgary	C. & V. (No. 1)		Dy.* tr. 4.
Kanata	14d	Red Deer	C. & L.	Erskine	Tue. Fri. 7.30.
Keep Hills	30	Edmonton	Ed. & P. G. (1)	Duffield	Mon. Fri. 7.00.
Kenex	18	Macleod	M. H. & N.	Monarch	Tue. Fri. 10.45.
Keoma	17	Calgary	Calgary		Dy. tr. 630, C.P.R.
Kersey	17	Calgary	Calgary	Irricana	Fri. 11.00.
Kessler	24	Red Deer	S. & H.	Czar	Peckham, Wed. 13.00.
Kevisville	20	Red Deer	Innisfail	Markerville	Dickson, Wed. Sat. 11.30
Kew	17c	Calgary	Calgary		Tue. Fri. 8.00.
Keystone	24	Strathcona	Wetaskiwin	Kenham Valley	Fri. 13.30.
Killam	14c	Strathcona	H. & W.		Dy. trs. 527, 528.
Killarney Lake	22a	Strathcona	Riv. & Wain.	Chauvin	Tue. Fri. 15.45.
Kimball	18a	Med. Hat	Lethbridge	Cardston	Tue. Sat. 14.00.
Kingman	21	Strathcona	Edmonton		Dy. tr. 12, G.T.P.
Kinmundy	15f	Med. Hat	S. & C.	Chinook	Mon. Thur. 7.30.
Kinnaird	20	Strathcona	Leduc	Calmar	Sat. 12.15.
Kinnondale	17	Med. Hat	Suffield Sta.	Lomond	Tue. Sat. 14.00.
Kinsella	22b	Strathcona	W. & E.		Dy. trs. 1, 2.
Kinuso	21	Edmonton	Edmonton		Mon. Thur. tr. 1, E. D. & B. C.
Kipp	18	Med. Hat	M. H. & N.		Dy. tr. 538.
Kippenville	18a	Med. Hat	Lethbridge	Milk River	Masinasin, Wed. Sat. 7.
Kirkcaldy	17c	Macleod	Calgary		Dy. tr. 512, C.P.R.
Kirriemuir	29	Red Deer	Coronation Kerr Robert		M. W. F. tr. 612, C.P.R. T. T. S. tr. 611, C.P.R.
Kitscoty	14	Victoria	N. B. & E.		Dy.* trs. 1, 2.
Klemme	26	Red Deer	Mun. & Cam.	Donalda	Mon. Fri. 11.45.
Kleskun Hill	21	Edmonton	Edmonton	Gr. Prairie	Tue. 7.00.
Knappen	18a	Med. Hat	Lethbridge	Coutts	St. Kilda, Wed. 7.00.
Knee Hill Valley	20	Red Deer	C. & E.	Innisfail	Wed. Sat. 8.00.

Office	Key No.	County	Distribution

OFFICE	KEY No.	COUNTY	DISTRIBUTION		
Knob Hill........	24	Strathcona....	Wetaskiwin.	Yeoford.	Mon [illegible]
Kopernick......	14c	Strathcona.	H. & W	Daysland.	Quarrel, Sat 8.00.
Krakow......	14	Victoria	N. B. & E	Mundare	Fri. 11.00

Office	Key No.	County	Distribution		

OFFICE	KEY No.	COUNTY	DISTRIBUTION		
Lac Bellevue.......	14	Victoria......	Vegreville......	Lafond.. ..	Fri. 13.30.
La Calmette.......	21	Edmonton.....	Edmonton.....	Legal	Tue. Sat. 10.45.
Lac la Biche.......	21	Victoria..	Edmonton..	Athabaska.....	Tue. 7.00.
Lac La Biche Sta...	21	Victoria.	Edmonton..	Athabaska.......	La. [illegible] Biche, Wed. 20.00
Lac la Nonne.......	21	Edmonton.....	Edmonton...	Busby.	Dunstable, Tue. Fri. 13.30.
Lacombe..........	20	Red Deer.....	C. & E.. C. & L.......		Dy.* trs. 524, 525. Dy. trs. 523, 526. Dy. tr. 529.
Lac Ste. Anne.....	21	Edmonton...	Edmonton.	. . . .	Wed. [illegible] tr. [illegible], C.N.R.
Lac St. Vincent....	14	Victoria..	Vegreville......	St. Paul de Metis,	T. T. S. 14.30.
Lafond............	14	Victoria...	Vegreville......	... ..	Dy. 8.00.
Lake de May.......	14c	Strathcona....	Camrose... ..	. .	Tues. Sat. 16.00.
Lake Eliza.......	14	Victoria.	Vermilion..	Hopkins.	Wed. 12.30.
Lake Geneva.......	14	Victoria. ..	N. B. & E.	Mannville.. ..	Fri. 12.30.
Lake Isle..........	30a	Edmonton.	E. & P. G...	Gainford.. .	[illegible]t. 8.00.
Lake Louise.......	17	Calgary.......	C. & V.. ..	.. ..	Dy.* trs. 4, 2 1.
Lake McGregor....	17	Med. Hat. ..	M. J. & C....	Gleichen.......	Mon. Thur. 7.30.
Lake Saskatoon....	21	Edmonton..	Edmonton.. .	Grande Prairie.	Wed. 7.00.
Lakesend..........	24	Red Deer......	S. & H... ...	Czar.....	Peckham, Wed. 13.00.
Lake Thelma.......	14d	Red Deer......	Coronation.....	.	Tue. Fri. 11.00.
Lamont...........	14	Victoria.......	N. B. & E.....	....	Dy. trs. 1, 2.
L'Amoureux........	14	Victoria.	Ft. Sask'n..	... .. .	T. T. S. 12.30.
Landonville........	14	Victoria...... .	Vermilion..	.. . .	Tue. 8.00.
Lanfine...........	15f	Med. Hat......	S. & C.........	Excel.	Wed. Sat. 9.30.
Langdon..........	17	Calgary........	M. J. & C.....	....	Dy. tr. 3, 4.
Lanuke...........	14	Victoria.......	Vegreville......	Two Hills.....	Tue. Sat. 14.30.
Lathom...........	17	Med. Hat......	M. J. & C.....	....	Dy. tr. 3.
Laurence..........	19	Macleod.......	Mac. & Cal.. Calgary......	Parkland......	Tue. Fri. 12.30.
Lavesta...........	20	Red Deer......	C. & E........	Ponoka........	Bluff Centre, Wed. Sat 8.00.
Lavoy............	14	Victoria.......	N. B. & E...	....	Dy.* trs. 1, 2.

OFFICE	KEY No.	COUNTY	DISTRIBUTION
'8 Linario			

Office	Key No.	County	Distribution		
Lawndale	17c	Med. Hat	Calgary / Lethbridg	Vulcan	Mon. Thur. 8.00.
Lawsonburg	15f	Med. Hat	S. & C	Craigmyle	Mon. 8 30, Thur. 9.00.
Lawton	21	Edmonton	Edmonton	Hanley	Belvedere, Tue Fri 14.30.
Leafland	20	Red Deer	Lacombe	Bentley	Gilby, Wed. 13.00.
Lealholme	22a	Strathcona	Riv. & Wain.	Chauvin	Wed. Sat. 17.00.
Leaman	30a	Edmonton	Ed. & P. G.		T. T. S [illegible]
Lea Park	14	Victoria	N B. & E	Kitscoty	Mon. Thu. 9.00.
Leasowe	21	Edmonton	Edmonton		Fri. 14.30.
Leavitt	18a	Med. Hat	Lethbridg	Cardston	Tue. Thu. Sat. 6.00.
Leduc	20	Strathcona	C. & E		Dy. trs. 523, 524, 525, 526.
Leeshore	14	Victoria	N. B. & E.	Lamont	Skaro, Sat 10.00.
Legal	21	Edmonton	Edmonton		M. W F. tr [illegible]; C.N.R.
Le Goff	14	Victoria	Vegreville	Durlingville	Wed. 7.00.
Leighton	14	Victoria	N. B. & E	Lloydminster	Tue. Sat. 7.00.
Leo	14d	Red Deer	C. & L.	Gadsby	Tue. Fri. 14.30.
Leslieville	20	Red Deer	Red Deer		M. W F. tr. 613, C.P.R.
*Lethbridge		Med. Hat	M. H. & [illegible]		Dy.* trs. 513, 514. Dy trs 511, 538.
			Calgary / Cardston / Coutts		Dy tr. 512 C.P.R. Dy. tr 530 C.P.R. Dy tr. 56[illegible] C.P.R.
Lindale	30a	Strathcona	Ed. & P. G.	Gainford	Burtonsville, Fri. 17.00.
Lineham	19	Macleod	Mac. & Cal. / Calgary	Okotoks	Tu. Thu. Sat. 14.00.
Linfield	21	Edmonton	Edmonton	Bussy	Mosside, Wed. Sat 12.00.
Little Plume	17	Med. Hat	Medicine Hat		Tue. Fri 7.15.
Little Volga	30a	Edmonton	Ed. & P. G.	Gainford	Tue. 12.00.
Livingstone	18	Macleod	M. H. & N.	Lundbreck	Tue. Fri. 8.15.
Lloyd's Hill	29	Red Deer	Coronation / Kerr Robert	Consort	Sat. 7.30.
Lobley	20	Red Deer	C. & E.	Olds	Mound, Tue. Fri. 14.30
Lochend	17	Calgary	C. & V. (No.1)	Cochrane	Fri. 8.30.

OFFICE	KEY No.	COUNTY	DISTRIBUTION		

2-

9.18 Lonira

Office	Key No.	County	Distribution		
Lochinvar........	20	Red Deer......	Lacombe..	..	Wed. Sat. 7.30.
Loch Sloy.......	19	Macleod..	Mac. & Cal.. Calgary.....	High River.	Tue. Fri. 11.00.
Lockhart..........	20	Red Deer..	Lacombe.	Bentley	Wed. 7.00. Sat. 12.30.
Logan....	22b	Strathcona..	Edmonton... W. & E..... Camrose..	Tofield..	Mon. Fri. 9.00.
Lomond...	17	Med. Hat....	~~Suffield Sta.~~		Mon. .. tr. 66 C.P.R.
Lonebutte......	15f	Med. Hat...	S. & C..	Hanna..	Mon. Thur. 8.00.
Lone Pine......	20	Red Deer	C. & E..	Didsbury..	Tue. Fri. 7.00.
Long Coulee.	18a	Med. Hat..	Lethbridge. Calgary...	Champion.	Tue. Fri. 13 00
Longview.....	19	Macleod.	Mac. & Cal. Calgary...	High River.	Tue. Sat. 7.00.
Lonira..	21	Edmonton.	Edmonton	Sangudo	Wed. Sat. 14.00.
Lougheed.....	14c	Strathcona...	H. & W		Dy. trs. 527. 528
Lorraine....	14d	Red Deer..	C. & L..	Castor.	T. T .. 8 00.
Lousana......	17c	Red Deer..	Calgary... Edmonton.	......	Dy. tr. 11, G. T. P. Dy. tr. 12. G. T. P.
Loveland.........	14c	Red Deer......	H. & W.....	Killam.	Tue. Sat. 8.00.
Lovettville...	30a	Edmonton..	Edson.		Wed. Fri., G. T. P. Alta. Coal Br.
Loyalist.	29	Red Deer.	Coronation.. Kerr Robert		M. W. F. tr. 612, C.P.R. T. T. S. tr. 611, C.P.R.
Lucky Strike.......	18a	Med. Hat......	Lethbridge...	Warner...	Goddard, Tue. Fri. 15.00
Lundbreck.....	18	Macleod.	M. H. & N.....	..	Dy. trs. 513, 514.
Lundemo....	21	Strathcona.....	Edmonton..	.	Mon. Fri. tr. 35, C.N.R.
Lunnford....	21	Edmonton..	Edmonton..	Clyde.	Dusseldorf, Tue Sat. 11.00.
Lusignan.......	21	Edmonton.....	Edmonton.....	~~New Lunnon~~..	~~Tue.~~ Sat. 9.00.
Luzan...........	14	Victoria.......	Vegreville......	Soda Lake.....	Fri. 15.30.
Lyndon.........	19	Macleod....	Mac. and Cal. Calgary..	Claresholm.....	Sat. 10.30.

Office	Key No.	County	Distribution		

OFFICE	KEY No.	COUNTY	DISTRIBUTION		
McDonaldville......	14	Strathcona...	N. B. & E.	Kitscoty...	Tue. Fri. 8.00.
McEwan.....	19	Macleod....	M. H. & N. Mac. & Cal. ~~Calgary~~....	Nanton..	Sat. 13.30.
McLaughlin........	14	Strathcona.....	N. B. & E..	Lloydminster...	Mon. Fri. 7.00.
McLennan.. ..	21	Edmonton.	Edmonton.	.	Mon. Thur. tr. 1, E. D & B. C.
McLeod Valley.....	30a	Edmonton..	Ed. & P. G.	Peers....	~~Fr.~~ 8.00.
McNally...........	17	Med. Hat.....	Bassano. Empress.	Steveville.	T. T. S. 8.00.
*Macleod..........	18	Macleod.	M. H. & N.... Mac. & Cal. Calgary.....	.	Dy. tr. 539. Dy.* trs. 513. 514. Dy. tr. 540. Dy tr. ~~538~~, C P R.
Magnolia..	30a	Edmonton.....	Ed. & P. G.	Entwistle.	Tue. Fri. 13.00.
Magrath...........	18a	~~Med Ha.~~	Lethbridge..		Dy. tr. 538, C.P.R.
Mahaska..	30a	Edmonton..	Ed. & P. G.	Peers	~~Fri~~ 8.00.
Majorville. ...	17	Med Hat......	M. J. & C.	Gleichen.	Mon. Thur. 7.30
Maleb...........	17	Med. Hat......	M. H. & N. (1).	Bow Island.	Tue. Fri. 15.00.
Malmo...........	24	Strathcona..	Wetaskiwin.	Lewisville..	M. W. F. 9.30.
Maloy....	14	Victoria.	Vegreville...	St. Paul de Met	Bordenave, Fri. 12.30.
Mance............	22b	Strathcona.....	W. & E....	Viking...	Tue. Fri. 13.00.
Manfred..........	21	Red Deer......	Edmonton... Camrose.....	Bashaw.	Tue. Fri. 9.00.
Manly............	30	Edmonton.....	Ed. & P. G....	Carvel Sta..	T. T. F. 8.30.
Mannville..........	14	Victoria.	N. B. & E..	.. ..	Dy. ex. Mon. trs. 1, 2.
Manola..........	21	Edmonton.....	Edmonton...	Busby..	Dunstable, Tue. Fri. 14.30.
Manyberries.......	17	Med. Hat......	~~M. H. & N. (1)~~.	~~Seven Persons~~..	Tue ~~7.00~~.
Markerville.......	20	Red Deer...	C. & E........	Innisfail...	Dy. 13.30.
Marlboro.........	30a	Edmonton...	Ed. & P. G.	.	Mon. Thur. tr 1. Tue. tr. 91.
Martins...........	22b	Strathcona.....	W. & E........	Holden... ...	Mon. Fri. 13.30.
Marwayne........	14	Victoria.......	N. B. & E...	Kitscoty......	Mon. Thu. 9.00.
Mary Lake.........	14	Victoria.. ...	Vermilion...	Maughan..	Wed. 8.00.
Masinasin..........	18a	Med. Hat..	Lethbridge.....	Milk River.....	Tue. Fri. 14.00.

OFFICE	KEY No.	COUNTY	DISTRIBUTION		

OFFICE	KEY No.	COUNTY	DISTRIBUTION		
Matthews Crossing..	30a	Edmonton.....	Ed. & P. G.	Entwistle....	Fri. 13.00.
Maughan........	14	Victoria.	Vermilion.. ..	.	Tue. Fri. 13.00.
Maunders..........	15f	Red Deer......	S. & C.....	Hanna...	Sat. 12.30.
Maybridge.........	21	Edmonton....	Edmonton.. ..	Fedorah..	Fri. 8.15.
Maybutt....	18a	Med. Hat......	Lethbridge...		Dy. via tr. 564, C.P.R.
Maycroft......	18	Macleod.....	M. H. & N...	Lundbreck.	Fri. 7.00.
Mayerthorpe.......	21	Edmonton...	Edmonton.	Sangudo..	Wed. Sat 14.00.
Mayton..	20	Red Deer....	C. & E..	Olds..	Tue. Fri. 8.00.
Mazeppa........	17c	Macleod...	Calgary..	.	Dy. via tr. 512, C.P.R.
Meadow Brook.. ..	21	Edmonton.	Edmonton.	Rochester..	Fri. 15.00.
Meadow Creek. ..	19	Macleod....	Mac. & Cal.. Calgary...	Claresholm	Tue. Sat. 14.00.
Meadowview.....	21	Edmonton..	Edmonton..	Battum.....	Wed. Sat. 16.00.
Meanook	21	Edmonton..	Edmonton...	.	M. W. F. via tr. 165, C.N.R.
Mecheche..........	15f	Red Deer....	S. & C...	.	Dy. tr. 24. Dy. ex. Mon. tr. 23.
*Medicine Hat..	17	Med. Hat....	M. J. & C.. M. H. & N...	.... .	Dy.* trs. 1, 2, 3, 4. Dy.* tr. 514. Dy. tr. 512.
Meeting Creek..	26	Red Deer.	Mun. & Cam..	.	M. W. F. tr. 35, T.T.S. tr. 36.
Melba.....	17c	Calgary.....	Calgary....	.	M. W F. 8.00.
Mellowdale.. ...	21	Edmonton.	Edmonton...	Dusseldorf,.	Tues. Sat. 8.00.
Mere.......	15f	Med. Hat....	S. & C.....	Alsask...	Sat. 8.30.
Merebeck	21	Edmonton. .	Edmonton.	.	Wed. Sat. tr 195, C.N.R.
Merl Bluff........	22a	Strathcona...	Riv. & Wain.	Dunn.	Fri. 9.00.
Merna............	14c	Strathcona.....	H. & W..	Sedgewick.	Tue. Fri. 8.00.
Merryland.........	15f	Med. Hat....	S. & C.. ...	Alsask.	Muhlbach, Sat. 16.00
Metiskow..........	24	Red Deer.	S. & H......	.....	Dy. tr. 51.
Mewassin..........	30	Edmonton...	Ed. & P. G. (1).	Duffield..	Tue. Fri. 10.00.
Michener........	15f	Red Deer...	S. & C.. ...	Delia ..	Wed. 13.00.
Midnapore..... ...	19	Calgary.....	Mac. & Cal... Calgary.......	... ..	Dy. trs. 537, 540. Dy. tr. 538, C.P.R.
Milk River........	18a	Med. Hat.....	Lethbridge.....	..	Dy. tr. 564, C.P.R.

OFFICE	KEY No.	COUNTY	DISTRIBUTION		

Office	Key No.	County	Distribution		
Millarville..	17c	Macleod...	Calgary..		Tue. Fri. 8.00.
Millerfield....	15f	Med. Hat....	S. & C.	Craigmyle	Dorothy, Tue. 11.10.
Millet......	20	Strathcona...	C. & E..		Dy. trs. 523, 524, 525, 526.
Milnerton........	20	Red Deer..	C. & E...	Innisfail..	Wed. Sat. 8.00.
Milo....	17	Med. Hat..	M. J. & C..	Gleichen...	Mon. Thur.
Minburn..........	14	Victoria.	N. B. & E.		Dy. trs. 1, 2.
Minda........	17	Med. Hat.....	M. H. & N. (1)	Seven Persons..	Tue., Fri. 7.00.
Ministik Lake......	22b	Strathcona...	W. & E....	Tofield.	T. T. S. 8.00.
Minnehik......	24	Strathcona.	Wetaskiwin.	Yeoford	Mon. 8.00.
Mirror..	21	Red Deer.	Edmonton.. Calgary...		Dy. tr. 12, G.T.P. Dy. tr. 11, G.T.P.
Mirror Landing.....	21	Edmonton..	Edmonton.		Mon. Thur. tr. 1, E. D. & B. C.
Mizpah.......	17	Med. Hat.	Bassano.	Brawford.	Tu 9.00
Monarch.....	18	Macleod.	M. H. & N. Lethbridge		Dy. trs. 513, 514. Dy. trs. 538, 539. Dy. 565 C.P.R.
Monitor..	29	Red Deer.	Coronation Kerr Robert...		M. W. F. tr. 612, C.P.R. T. T. S. tr. 611, C.P.R.
Monvel.......	26	Red Deer..	Mun. & Cam..	Red Willow.	Mon. Fri. 16.00.
Mooswa........	14	Victoria..	N. B. & E.	Kitscoty.	Lea Park, Tue. Fri. 9.00.
Morinville....	21	Edmonton..	Edmonton..		M. W. F. tr. 165, C.N.R. T. T. S. tr. 169, C.N.R.
Morley......	17	Calgary....	C. & V. (No. (1)		Dy. trs. 3, 4.
Morningside........	20	Red Deer...	C. & E...		Dy. trs. 523, 524.
Morrin..........	26	Red Deer...	Mun. & Cam..		M. W. F. tr. 35 T. T. S. tr. 36.
Mortonmoor......	14	Victoria	N. B. & E.	Lamont..	Downing. Fri. 12.15.
Mosside.......	21	Edmonton..	Edmonton..	Busby.	Belvedere, Tue. Fri. 14.30.
Mossleigh......	17c	Macleod....	Calgary..... Lethbridge..	Blackie...	T. T. S. 8.00.
Mound.......	20	Red Deer......	C. & E...	Olds......	Tue. Fri. 8.00.
Mountain House....	20	Red Deer......	C. & E....	Bowden......	Tue. Fri. 14.00.
Mountain Park.....	30a	Edmonton....	Edson..		Wed. Fri., G.T.P., Alta. Coals Br.

OFFICE	KEY No.	COUNTY	DISTRIBUTION		

OFFICE	KEY No.	COUNTY	DISTRIBUTION		
Mountain View.....	18a	Med. Hat. ..	Lethbridge...	Cardston..	Tue. Thu. Sa . 6.00.
Moyerton.........	14	Strathcona..	N. B. & E.	Kitscoty.	Tue. Fri. 8.00.
Muhlbach.........	15f	Med. Hat...	S. & C...	Alsask..	Sat. 8.30.
Muirhead.....	19	Macleod.	Nanton..	.	Sat. 14.00.
Mulga............	14	Victoria..	N. B. & E.	Mannville.	Sat. 9.00.
Mulhurst..........	20	Strathcona..	C. & E..	Millet	{Patience. {Wed. Sat. 13.00.
Mundare.	14	Victoria..	N. B. & E.	.	Dy. trs 1, 2
Munson.........	15f	Med. Hat.	{S. & C.... {Mun. & Cam.	.	{Dy tr. 24. {Dy x. Mon. tr. M. W. F. tr. 35.
Murray Valley.....	20	Red Deer.	C. & E.	Olds.	Sat. 15.00.
Musidora..........	14	Victoria.	Vegreville...	Duvernay.	Mon. Fri. 13.30.
Mussel.....	30a	Edmonton.	Ed. & P. G.	Peers...	Fri. 15.00.
Myleen.....	15f	Med. Hat..	S. & C..	Benton Station.	Tue. Fri. 11.00.
Myrnam...........	14	Victoria.	N. B. & E.	Mannville..	Sat. 7.00.
Myrtle Creek......	14	Victoria.	Fort Sask'n.	.	Tue. Fri. 8.00.

Office	Key No.	County	Distribution		

OFFICE	KEY No.	COUNTY	DISTRIBUTION		
Nakamun	21	Edmonton	Edmonton	Busby	Sion, Tue. Fri. 1 [illegible]
Namaka	17	Med. Hat	M. J. & C.		Dy. tr. 3, 4.
Namao	21	Edmonton	Edmonton.		M. W. F. 6.30.
Nanton	19	Macleod	Mac. & Cal. ~~Calgary~~ M. H. & N.		Dy. trs. 537 540. Dy tr 538 C.P.R. Dy. tr. 539.
Nateby	~~17~~	~~Med. Hat~~	~~Bassano~~ ~~Empress~~	~~Steveville.~~	~~Tue. Fri. 11.00~~
Nathella	15f	Med. Hat.	S. & C	Usask.	Tue. Fri. 14.00.
Naughton Glen	14	Victoria	N. B. & E.	Mannville.	Sat 7.00.
Needmore	17	Med. Hat	M. H & N (1).	Seven Persons	Manybe[illegible] Wed. Sat. 13 1[illegible]
Neerlandia	21	Edmonton	Edmonton.	Westlock	Mellowdale, Tue [illegible]
Nemiskam	~~17~~ 10	Med. Hat.	~~M. H. & [illegible] (1)~~	Burdett	Tue. F[illegible] 8.00.
Nestor	22b	[illegible]athcona	[illegible]		M. W. F. tr T T.
Nestow	21	Edmonton	Edmonton		M. W. F. tr 165 C.N.R.
Neuchatel	14c	Red Deer.	H. & W	Sedgewick.	Tue. Fri. 8.00.
Neutral Hills	24	~~Red Deer~~	S. & H.	Czar	Wed. 9.00.
Neutral Valley	29	Red Deer	Coronation Kerr Robert	Consort	Sat 7.30.
Nevis	14d	Red Deer	C. & L.		Dy. trs. 529, 530.
New Brigden	15i	Red Deer	S. & C.	Oyen	Fri. 8.00.
Newburg	17	Med. Hat	M. J. & C.	Irvine	Tue. Fri. 7.00.
New Dayton	18a	Med. Hat	Lethbridge.		Dy. tr. 564.
New Hill	20	Red Deer	C. & E.	Innisfail.	Markerville, Wed. 13.30.
New Lindsay	14	Strathcona	N. B. & E.	Lloydminster	Mon. Fri. 7.00.
New Lunnon	21	Edmonton	Edmonton		M. W. F. 6.30.
New Norway	21	Strathcona	Edmonton Camrose		Dy. [illegible]. 12, G.T.P.
New Oxley	19	Macleod	Mac. & Cal. Calgary	Claresholm	Tue. Sat. 15.15.
New Sarepta	21	Strathcona	Edmonton Camrose.		Mon. Fri. tr. 35, C.N.R. Tue. Sat. tr. 3[illegible] C.N.R.
Nightingale	17	~~Med. Hat~~	Bassano		[illegible] tr [illegible]67, C.P.R.
Nilrem	24	Strathcona	S. & H.	Amisk	Mon. Fri. 8.30.

OFFICE	KEY No.	COUNTY	DISTRIBUTION	
Niton	30a	W. Ed.		

OFFICE	KEY No.	COUNTY	DISTRIBUTION		
Niobe..	21	Edmonton	Edmonton..	Gr. Prairie	Wed. [illegible]00.
Nisbet........	20	Red Deer....	C. & E......	Bowden..	Fri. 12.30.
Nobleford.........	18a	Macleod......	Lethbridge.... Calgary.....	..	Dy. tr. 511, C.P.R. Dy. tr. 512, C.P.R.
Nordegg. ...	26	Red Deer.	Red Deer.	Rocky Mt House	Tue. Fri. tr. 183, [illegible]
Normandeau.	14	Victoria.	Vegreville	Grandin.	Fri. 1[illegible].00.
Northbank.	14	Victoria..	~~N. B. &~~	Lamont.	Pakan, Fri. ~~9.00~~.
North Cooking Lake	22b	Strathcona..	W. & E.	...	Dy. tr. 2.
North Edmonton..	14	Edmonton.	N. B. & F	...	Dy. tr. 1, 2
Northern Valley...	14	Victoria	Vermilion.	.	Tue. Fri. 13.00.
North Fork..	18	Macleod.	M. H. & N.	Cowley..	Fri. 13.30.
Northleigh..	30a	Edmonton.	Ed. & P. G.	Gainford.	Tomahawk, Tue 1[illegible].00.
North Vermilion..	21	Edmonton...	Edmonton..	Peace River Crossing..	Ex. Apr. & Nov. 1st each month.
Norton.......	17	Med. Hat......	M. J. & C.	Coleridge	Tue. Fri. 13.00.
Noyes Crossing.....	21	Edmonton...	Edmonton...	Onoway	Wed. Sat. 13.30.
Nugent........	20	Strathcona...	C. & E..	Ponoka..	Bluff Centre, W. Sat. 8.00.

OFFICE	KEY No	COUNTY	DISTRIBUTION		

Office	Key No.	County	Distribution		
Ohaton	14c	Strathcona	H. & W.		Dy. tr
Okotoks	19	Macleod	Calgary Mac. & Cal.		Dy. tr. 538, C.P.R. Dy. trs. 537, 540.
Olds	20	Red Deer	C. & E.		Dy. trs. 523, 526. Dy. *trs. 525, 524.
Olsen Creek	18	Macleod	Macleod.		Sat. 9.00.
Onefour	17	Med. Hat	M. H. & N. (1)	Seven Persons	Manyberries, Wed. 13.00.
Onoway	21	Edmonton	Edmonton		Wed. Sat. tr. 195, C.N.R.
Opal	14	Edmonton	Fort Sask'n		Tue. Fri. 8.00.
Orbindale	22b	Strathcona	W. & E.	Irma	Fri. 14.00.
Orton	18	Macleod	Macleod		T.T.S. 11.00.
Orvilton	14	Victoria	Vermilion	Hopkins	Wed. 14.00.
Ouelletteville	17	Med. Hat	M. J. & C.	Cluny Station	M. W. F. S. 11.00.
Owlseye Lake	14	Victoria	Vegreville	St. Paul de Metis	Fri. 11.00.
Oxville	14	Strathcona	N. B. & E.	Lloydminster	Mon. Fri. 7.00.
Oyen	15f	Med. Hat	S. & C.		Dy. trs. 23, 24.

OFFICE	KEY No.	COUNTY	DISTRIBUTION		

OFFICE	KEY No.	COUNTY	DISTRIBUTION		
Paddle River	21	Edmonton	Edmonton	Westlock	Dusseldorf, Tue. Sat. 11.00.
Padstow	21	Edmonton	Edmonton	Wan[illegible]kville	Thur. 9.00.
Pakan	14	Victoria	N. B. & E.	Lamont	Andrew, Tue. Fri. 7.30.
Pakowki	~~17~~	Med. Hat	~~M. H. & N.~~ (1)	Seven Persons	Needmore, Thur. 8.00.
Pancras	17	Med. Hat	Bassano Empress		Mon. Thur. tr. 670, C.P.R. Tue. Fri. tr. 671, C.P.R.
Pandora	17	Med. Hat	Bassano Richdale	Favor	T. T. S. 9.40.
Paradise Valley	14	Strathcona	N. B. & E.	Lloydminster	Mon. Fri. 7.00.
Park Court	30a	Edmonton	Ed. & P. G.	Entwistle	Fri. 13.00.
Parkland	19	Macleod	Mac. & Cal. Calgary		Dy. trs. 537, 540. Dy. tr. 538. C.P.R.
Parr	15f	Med. Hat	S. & C.	Hanna	Mon. Thur. 8.00.
Parvella	17	Med. Hat	Bassanao. Empress.	Atlee	Tue. Fri. 12.00.
Pashley	17	Med. Hat	M. J. & C.		Dy. trs.
Passburg	18	Macleod	M. H. & N.		Dy. trs. 513, 514.
Pathfinder	14	Victoria	N. B. & E.	Mannville	Myrnam, Sat. ~~10.30~~
Patience	20	Strathcona	C. & E.	Millet	Wed. Sat. 9.00.
Paxson	21	Victoria	Edmonton	Athabaska	Tue. 8.00.
Payndale	14	Strathcona	N. B. & E.	Mannville	Cotterview, Sat. 10.4[illegible]
Pearce	~~18~~	Macleod	~~M. H. & N.~~		Dy. tr. 538
Peat	14	Victoria	Vermilion	Angle Lake	Sat. 9.00.
Peavine	21	Edmonton	Edmonton	Roydale	Thur. 7.00.
Peace River ~~Crossing~~	21	Edmonton	Edmonton		M. Thur. tr. 1, E. D. & B. C.
Peckham	24	~~Red Deer~~	S. & H.	Czar	Wed. 9.00.
Peerless	17	Med. Hat	Bassano Empress	Jenner	Thur. 13.00.
Peers	30a	Edmonton	Ed. & P. G.		T. T. S. trs. 3, 4.
Peguis	14	Victoria	Vermilion		Tue. Fri. 13.00.
Pekisko	19	Macleod	Mac. & Cal., Calgary	High River	Tue. Fri. 11.00.

OFFICE	KEY No.	COUNTY	DISTRIBUTION		

OFFICE	KEY No.	COUNTY	DISTRIBUTION		
Pembina	21	Edmonton	Edmonton	Clyde	Westlock, Mon. Fri. 15.00.
Pemburton Hill	20	Strathcona	C. & E.	Leduc	Telfordville, Thu. 10.30.
Pendant d'Oreille	18a	Med. Hat	Lethbridge	Warner	Altorado, Wed. Sat. 8.00.
Penhold	20	Red Deer	C. & E.		Dy. trs. 523, 524, 525, 562
Peno	14	Victoria	N. B. & E.	Lamont	Wed. 13.00, Sat. 8.00.
Perbeck	17c	Red Deer	Calgary Edmonton	Huxley	Mon. Fri. 16.15.
Perryvale	21	Edmonton	Edmonton		Mon. Fri. tr. 16, C.N.R.
Phillips	22b	Strathcona	W. & E.		M. W. F. tr. 1. T. T. S. tr. 2.
Pibroch	21	Edmonton	Edmonton		M. Th. tr. 1, E. D. & B. C.
Pickardville	21	Edmonton	Edmonton	Westlock	Tue. Sat. 11.30.
Picture Butte	18a	Med. Hat	Lethbridge		M. W. F. 14.00.
Pincher Creek	18	Macleod	M. H. & N.		Dy. *trs. 513, 514.
Pincher Station	18	Macleod	M. H. & N.		Dy. trs. 513, 514.
Pine Canyon	19	Macleod	De Winton	Gladys	Thu. 15.00.
Pine Creek	14	Victoria	Fort Sask'n		Tue. Fri. 8.00.
Pine Lake	20	Red Deer	C. & E.	Penhold	Wed. Sat. 7.45.
Pinhorn	18a	Med. Hat	Lethbridge	Coutts	Aden, Wed. 10.00.
Pioneer	26	Red Deer	Mun. & Cam.	Red Willow	Wed. Sat. 14.30.
Pirmez Creek	17c	Calgary	Calgary	Spring Bank	Wed. 14.00.
Pitcox	20	Red Deer	Red Deer		M. W. F. tr. 613, C.P.R.
Plain Lake	14	Victoria	Vegreville	Lanuke	Sat. 15.00.
Plamondon	21	Victoria	Edmonton	Athabaska	Tue. 8.00.
Pleasant View	17	Med. Hat	M. H. & N. (1)	Winnifred	Wed. Sat. 8.00.
Pleasington	14c	Strathcona	H. & W.	Killam	Tue. Sat. 8.00.
Pocahontas	30a	Edmonton	Ed. & P. G.		Mon. Thur. tr. 1. Tue. Fri. tr. 2. Tue. tr. 91. Sun. tr. 92.
Poe	22b	Strathcona	W. & E.		Dy. tr. 2.
Pokehasset	20	Strathcona	C. & E.	Leduc	Telfordville, Thur. 10.30.
Pollockville	17	Med. Hat	Bassano Empress	Steveville	T. T. S. 8.00.

OFFICE	KEY No.	COUNTY	DISTRIBUTION		

OFFICE	KEY No.	COUNTY	DISTRIBUTION		
Pollux	14d	Red Deer	C. & L.	Castor	Fri. 12.00.
Ponoka	20	Red Deer	C. & E.		Dy.* trs. 524, 525. Dy. 523, 526.
Power House	30a	Edmonton	Gainford	Rocky Rapids	Wed. 12.00.
Prague	22b	Strathcona	W. & E.	Viking	Tue. Fri. 13.30.
Priddis	17c	Macleod	Calgary		Tue. Fri. 8.00.
Primula	14	Victoria	N. B. & E.	Islay	Greenlawn, Fri. 16.00.
Prospect Valley	22a	Strathcona	Riv. & Wain.	Edgerton St'n.	Tue. Fri. 14.30.
Prospy	17	Med. Hat	M. H. & N. (1)	Winnifred	Wed. Sat. 8.00.
Provost	24	Strathcona	S. & H.		Dy. trs. 51, 52.
Puffer	24	Strathcona	S. & H.	Amisk	M. F. 8.30.
Purple Springs	17	Med. Hat	M. H. & N. (1)		Dy. trs. 511, 512.

Office	Key No.	County	Distribution	

Office	Key No.	County	Distribution		
Quarrel..........	14c	Strathcona.....	H & W.........	Daysland...	Tue. Fri. 12.00.
Queenstown	17	Med. Hat......	M. J. & C.	Gleichen	Mon. Thur. 7.30.

OFFICE	KEY No.	COUNTY	DISTRIBUTION		

OFFICE	KEY No.	COUNTY	DISTRIBUTION		
Radway Centre.....	14	Victoria.....	Ft. Sask'n.	Myrtle Cr'k..	Tue. Fri. 19.00.
Rainbow...........	15f	Med. Hat...	S. & C... Bassano.	Craigmyle.....	Lawsonburg, Thur. 15.00
Rainy Hills........	17	Med. Hat....	Bassano..		Mon. Thur. tr. 670, C.P.R.
Raley........	18a	Med. Hat......	Lethbridge.....	......	T. T. S. tr. 538, C.P.R.
Ranching........	14d	Red Deer.....	C. & L.........	Gadsby....	Tue. Fri. 14.30.
Ranchville........	17	Med. Hat....	M. H. & N. (1).	Seven Persons.	Glen Banner, Wed. 10.30.
Ranfurly...........	14	Victoria..	N. B. & E..	......	Dy.* trs. 1, 2.
Rapid Narrows.....	17	Med. Hat..	M. J. & C......	Pashley..	Waddington, Tue. 13.00.
Raven...........	20	Red Deer.	C. & E....	Innisfail..	Markerville, T. T. [illegible]00
Ravine...........	30a	Edmonton...	Ed. & P. G.	Junkins....	Fri. 8.00.
Raymond........	18a	Med. Hat....	Lethbridge...	..	Dy. tr. 538, C.P.R.
Rearville........	15f	Med. Hat.....	S. & C.	Chinook..	Wed. 8.00.
Redcliff............	17	Med. Hat....	M. J. & C...	..	Dy. trs. 3, 4, 1.
Red Deer......	20	Red Deer..	C. & E.........	..	Dy. trs. 523, 526. Dy.* 524, 525.
Redland........	15f	Med. Hat...	S. & C.. ...	..	Dy. tr. 24.
Red Lodge...	20	Red Deer..	C. & E.........	Bowden..	Tue. Fri. 1[illegible]
Redwater.........	14	Victoria.	Fort Sask'n	..	Tue. Fri. 8.00.
Red Willow....	26	Red Deer.	Mun. & Cam...	..	M. W. F. tr. 35. T. T. S. tr. 36.
Reid Hill........	17c	Macleod	Calgary... Lethbridge	Vulcan..	Mon. Thur. 8.00
Reist........	15f	Red Deer.	Youngstown.	..	M. W. F. 13.00.
Retlaw.........	17	Med. Hat...	Suffield Sta.	..	Mon. Fri. tr. 665, C.P.R.
Rexboro........	30	Edmonton...	Wabamun..	..	Tue. Sat. 8.00.
Ribstone..........	22a	Strathcona..	Riv. & Wain..	....	Dy. tr. 2.
Rice..............	19	Macleod....	High River.....	Pekisko.....	Sat. 13.00.
Richdale..........	15f	Med. Hat......	S. & C........ Bassano.	..	Dy. ex. Mon. trs. [illegible], 24. M. W. F. 8.00.
Rich Valley........	21	Edmonton..	Edmonton..	Busby.	Dunstable, Tue. Fri. 13.30.
Ricinus...........	20	Red Deer......	Red Deer.....	Rocky Mt. House.	Caroline, Fri. 13.30.

OFFICE	KEY No.	COUNTY	DISTRIBUTION		

OFFICE	KEY No.	COUNTY	DISTRIBUTION		
Riddellvale	15f	Med. Hat	S. & C.	Cereal	Tue. Fri 7.00.
Ridgeclough	14	Strathcona	N. B. & E.	Lloydminster.	Tue Sa 8.00.
Rife	14	Victoria	Vegreville	St. Paul de Metis.	Tue Sat. 7.00.
Rimbey	20	Red Deer	Lacombe		Dy. 8.00.
Rising Sun	14	Strathcona	N. B. & E.	Lloydminster.	Mon. Fri. 7.00.
Riverbow	17	Med. Hat	Suffield Sta.	Retlaw	Mon Fri. 14.00.
River Course	14	Strathcona	N. B. & E.	Lloydminster.	Tue Sat. 8.00.
Riverton	14	Victoria	N. B. & E.	Kitscoty	Lea Park, Mon. Thu. 16.30.
Riviere Castor	14	Victoria	Vegreville	Durlingville.	Thu. 13.00.
Riviere Qui Barre	21	Edmonton	Edmonton.		M. W. F tr. 16[illegible] C.N.R. T. T. S tr. 169, C N.R
Rochester	21	Edmonton	Edmonton.		M. W F. tr. 165, C N.R.
Rockyford	15f	Med. Hat	S. & C.		Dy [illegible]
Rocky Mountain House	20	Red Deer	Red Deer		M. W. F. tr. 613, C.P.R.
Rocky Rapids	30a	Edmonton	Ed. & P. G	Gainford.	Tomahawk, Tue. 13.00.
Rocky View	17c	Calgary	Calgary		Wed. Sat. 14.30.
Rodino	14	Strathcona	N. B. & E	Minburn	Sat. 12.00.
Rollinson	15f	Red Deer	Youngstown	Wastina.	Sat. 8.30.
Ronan	30a	Edmonton	Ed. & P. G	Junkins	Fri. 8.00.
Roros	22a	Strathcona.	Riv. & Wain.	Chauvin	Fri. 15.15.
Rosebeg	17	Med. Hat	Medicine Hat.		Tue. Fri. 7.30.
Rosebud Creek	15f	Med. Hat	S. & C.		M W. F. tr. 24. T. T. S. tr. 23.
Rosedale	15f	Med. Hat	S. & C.		Dy. tr. 24.
Roseglen	17	Med. Hat	[illegible]	Pashley	Mon. 9.00.
Roselea	21	Edmonton	Edmonton	[illegible]	Mosside Sat. 13.00.
Rose Lynn	17	Med. Hat	Bassano. Richdale		M. W. F. 8.00.
Rosemead	17	Med. Hat	Suffield Sta.	Travers	Tue. Sat. 9.30.

OFFICE	KEY No.	COUNTY	DISTRIBUTION		

Office	Key No.	County	Distribution		
Rosevear....	30a	Edmonton..	Ed. & P. G	....	T. T. S. trs 3, 4.
Ross Creek.........	22b	Victoria....	Tofield.	......	Mon. Fri. 9.00.
Rossington.........	21	Edmonton......	Edmonton..	Clyde.	Hazel Bluff. Mon. Fri. 18.00.
Rosyth............	24	Strathcona..	S. & H..	......	Dy. tr. 52.
Round Hill.........	14	Strathcona.....	Vegreville..... Camrose....	....	T. T. S. tr. 157, C.N.R. M. W. F. tr. 158, C.N.R.
Round Up........	19	Macleod....	Mac. & Cal.. Calgary.....	Granum..	Wed. Sat. 12.45.
Rowley Station.....	26	Red Deer......	Mun. & Cam...	..	M. W. F. tr. [illegible] T. T. S. tr. [illegible]6
Royalview..........	18a	Med. Hat. ..	Lethbridge.....	..	Dy. 10.00.
Roydale.........	21	Edmonton.. .	Edmonton....	Sangudo.	Wed. Sat. 14.00.
Ruddington......	23	Med. Hat..	Empress......		Fri. 13.30.
Rumsey...........	26	Red Deer.....	Mun. & Cam..		M. W. F. tr. 35 T. T. S. tr. 36.
Rusylvia.........	14	Victoria.....	Vermilion...	.	Tue. 8.00.
Ryley......	22b	Strathcona.	W. & E......	......	Dy. trs. 1, 2.

OFFICE	KEY No.	COUNTY	DISTRIBUTION

Office	Key No.	County	Distribution		
St. Albert..........	21	Edmonton...	Edmonton...	...	M. W. F. tr. 165, C.N.R. T. T. S. tr. 169, C. N. R.
St. Edouard........	14	Victoria.......	Vegreville......	St. Paul de Metis..	Mon. Fri. 13.30.
St. Kilda..........	18a	Med. Hat.	Lethbridge.	Coutts..	Tue. Sat. [illegible]
St. Lina...........	14	Victoria	Vegreville	St. Paul des Metis...	Therien, Mon. Fri. 11.00
St. Paul de Metis...	14	Victoria.	Vegreville..	..	Dy. 8.00.
Sacred Heart.......	14	Victoria.	N. B. & E	Lamont.	M. Th. 7.00.
Saddle Lake........	14	Victoria.	N. B. & E Vegreville	Lamont. Duvernay.	M. Th. 7.00 Tue. 8.00.
Sage Creek....	17	Med. Hat.	M. H. & N. (1).	Seven Persons..	Manyberries, Wed. 13.00.
Saltaux.......	14	Strathcona..	N. B. & E.	Mannville..	Fri. 14.00.
Sampsonton........	17	Calgary..	C. & E. (No. 1)	Crossfield...	Tue. Fri. 13.00.
Sandstone..........	19	Macleod..	Mac. & Cal..	. . .	Dy. trs. 537, 540.
Sangudo...........	21	Edmonton.	Edmonton.		Wed. Sat. tr. 195, C.N.R.
Sarcee Butte.......	17c	Red Deer.....	Calgary...... Edmonton...	Three Hills..	Ghost Pine Creek, Tue. Sat. 10.30.
Saskalta.........	29	Red Deer. ..	Coronation.	Wilhelmina	Tue. [illegible] 00.
Sawdy........	21	Edmonton.	Edmonton.	Athabaska. .	Sat. 13.00.
Sawridge........ .	21	Edmonton..	Edmonton.		Mon. Thur. tr. 1. E. D. & B. C.
Schuler............	17	Med. Hat......	M. J. & C ..	Irvine..... ...	Tue. Fri. 8.00.
Scollard..	26	Red Deer....	Mun. & Cam..	....	M. W. F. tr. 35. T. T. S. tr. 36.
Scotfield...........	15f	Med. Hat......	S. & C.. ..	. . .	Dy. ex. Mon. tr. 23.
Scottsdale..........	24	Strathcona.....	Wetaskiwin.	Brightview...	Sat. 13.30.
Seal.....	15f	Med. Hat.. ...	S. & C.	Oyen.........	Fri. 8.00.
Seba Beach... .	30a	Edmonton..	Ed. & P. G.	Gainford .	Tue. Fri. 9.00.
Sedalia............	15f	Red Deer.....	S. & C..	Cereal...... ..	Tue. Fri. 7.00.
Sedgewick.........	14c	Strathcona.....	H. & W..	... ...	Dy. trs. 527, 528.
Seebe..............	17	Calgary........	C. & V. (1)..	....	Dy.* tr. 4.
Seven Persons......	17	Med. Hat....	M. H. & N. (1)	.. . . .	Dy.* trs. 513. Dy. trs. 511, 5[illegible] 14.
Sexsmith..........	21	Edmonton.....	Edmonton..	Peace R. Cross	Wed. Sat. 8.00.

OFFICE	KEY No.	COUNTY	DISTRIBUTION	

Office	Key No.	County	Distribution		
Seymour	21	Edmonton	Edmonton	Busby	Tu. Fri. [illegible].00.
Shaftesbury	21	Edmonton	Edmonton	Peace R. ~~Cross~~	~~Wed. S~~ [illegible] 00.
Shalka	14	Victoria	Vegreville	[illegible]arwick	Hairy Hill. Wed. 8.00.
Shamrock Valley	14	Victoria	Vermilion	Elk Point	16 30.
Shandleigh	17	Med. Hat	Bassano. Empress	[illegible]ville	Tue Fri. 10.00.
Shandro	14	Victoria	N. B. & E.	Lamont	Mon. Thur. 7.00
Sheerness		~~Med. Hat~~	Bassano Richdal		[illegible] 8 00.
Shepard	17c	Calgary	Calgary		[illegible] 0, C. P.R
Shepenge	14	Victoria	Vegreville	W[illegible]rwick	Ha[illegible] H ll, Wed 8.00
Shining Bank	30a	Edmonton	Ed. & P.	Peers	Fri. 8.00.
Shoal Creek	21	Edmonton	Edmonton	Clyde	Du[illegible] [illegible] 1[illegible].30.
Sibbald	15f	Med. Hat	S. & C.		[illegible] Mon. [illegible] 24.
Sidcup	14	Strathcona	N. B. & E.	Kitscot	Mo[illegible] 12 00.
Sideview	14	Victoria	Vegreville	[illegible] Paul de Metis.	Therien-St. Lina, Wed. 15.00.
Siebertville	17	Calgary	C. & E. No.	Carstairs	Tue Fri. 8.00.
Simons Valley	17c	Calgary	Calgary		T.T.S [illegible].00.
Sion	21	Edmonton	Edmonton	[illegible]sby	Tue. Fri 8.00.
Skaro	14	Victoria	N. B. & E	Lamont	8.00.
Slawa	14	Victoria	Vermilion	[illegible]eguis	[illegible]ed. 10.00.
Smoky Lake	14	Victoria	N. B. & E.	Lamont	[illegible]ak[illegible]n, Tue Fr. 14.00.
Smoky Lake Centre	14	Victoria	Fort Sask'n.	[illegible]ine Cre[illegible]	[illegible]d. 10.00.
Sniatyn	14	Victoria	N. B. & E.	Lamont	[illegible]ndrew, Tue Fri. 7 [illegible]0.
Social Plains	17 ~~28~~	Med. Hat	[illegible]		[illegible] ~~13.30~~.
Soda Lake	14	Victoria	Vegreville	[illegible]arwick	Tue. Fri. 10.30.
Solberg	15f	Med. Hat	S. & C.	Stanmore	Baraca, Sat. 8.00.
Sounding Lake	29	Red Deer	Coronation. Kerr Robert.	Monitor.	Wed. 14.00.
South Ferriby	14	Victoria	N. B. & E.	Lloydminster	Tue. Sat 7.00.
Spennymoor	15f	Med. Hat	S. & C.	Excel	Cappon, Thu. 14.15.
Spirit River	21	Edmonton	Edmonton	~~McLennan~~	Tue. Fri ~~12.00~~.

OFFICE	KEY No.	COUNTY	DISTRIBUTION	

Office	Key No.	County	Distribution		
Spitfire Lake....	21	Edmonton..	Edmonton	Gr Prair.	W.d. 7 [illegible]
Spring Bank......	17c	Calgary........	Calgary....	.. ....	Wed. Sat. [illegible] 00.
Spring Coulee......	18a	Med. Hat.....	Lethbridge..		D[illegible] tr[illegible] C.P R.
Springdale......	20	Strathcona...	C. & E.	Ponoka......	[illegible] Fri. 7.00.
Spring Lake........	14c	Strathcona....	H. & W.....	Daysland....	M.W.F. 1[illegible].00.
Spring Park........	14	Victoria..	Vermilion	Elk Poin[illegible]	7 [illegible]
Spring Point.......	18	Macleod......	Macleod .	.....	[illegible]
Springridge......	18	Macleod......	M. H. & N..	Pincher Creek.	[illegible]hburn Tr Fri 11.00.
Sprucefield......	14	Victoria	Fort [illegible]	[illegible]	[illegible]
Spruce Grove.....	30	Edmonton..	[illegible]d. & P. [illegible]		Sun. [illegible] 1. T[illegible] Tu[illegible]
Stafford Village.	18a	Med. Hat...	Lethbridg[illegible]		10.00.
Stainsleigh....	24	Red Deer....	S. & H. ..	Ha[illegible]	[illegible]
Standard. ...	17	Med. Hat..	.Bassano ..	.	[illegible] 7 P.M.
Stand Off.........	18	Macleod....	Macleod.. .	..	Dr[illegible] . 14.00.
Stanger	21	Edmonton	Edmonton	Moreb[illegible]ck	[illegible] 14.00

Or…	K y No.	…UNTY	DISTRIBUTION		

OFFICE	KEY No.	COUNTY	DISTRIBUTION		
Stewartwyn.......	26	Red Deer....	Mun. & Cam.	...	Fri. tr. 3[illegible]
Stirling..........	18a	Med. Hat......	Lethbridge....	.. ..	Dy. tr. 564 C.P.R
Stocks...........	21	Victoria......	Edmonton....	Athabaska....	Tue. [illegible].00.
Stokkeville......	14	Victoria.......	N. B. & E.	[illegible]orradai[illegible]	Tue. [illegible] ri 7 00.
Stonelaw.........	26	Red Deer....	Mun. & Cam..	Big V[illegible]le	Tu[illegible] [illegible]t. 14.00.
Stony Plain...	[illegible]0	Edmonton..	Ed. [illegible] P. G. (1)		[illegible]an. W[illegible] d[illegible] 1. T. T. [illegible] W[illegible]d. S[illegible] Mon. tr. 92, Tue. tr. 91
Stoppington.......	15	Med. Hat .	C	[illegible]anmore.	[illegible] [illegible]0.
*Strathcona....	[illegible]0	Str[illegible]thcona...	.. ...		
Strathmore. ...	17	Calgary.....	M. J. & C.		Dy [illegible]rs. 3, 4.
Streamstown... ...	14	[illegible]tor[illegible]....	B. [illegible]	[illegible]lo[illegible]dminster..	Tu[illegible] 7.00
Strome...	14[illegible]	Strathcona .	H. & W.		[illegible] 528
Stry.........	14	Victoria.	N B. & E.	Lamont ...	[illegible]red [illegible] Tue. Fri. 14.00.
Sturgeonville.....	14	Edmonton.. ..	Fort S[illegible]k'n.		Tue. Fri. 8.00.
Suffield Station....	17	Med. Hat....	M. J. & C..	....	Dy trs. 3, 4.
Sullivan Lake.	14d	Red Deer....	C. & L....	[illegible]astor... ..	[illegible]. W. F. [illegible]00.
Sulphur Springs. .	24	[illegible]rath[illegible]n	[illegible]... ..	Provost... ...	[illegible]. T. [illegible]
Summerview... ..	18	Macleod...	[illegible]. H. N...	Pinch[illegible] Sta[illegible]on	Tu[illegible] Fri. 11 [illegible].
Sunbeam...	26	Red Deer...	[illegible]	Morrin	[illegible]d. 10.1[illegible]
Sundial......	18[illegible]	Med. Hat..	Lethbridge....		Mo[illegible] W[illegible] 14.00
Sundre........ .	20	Red Deer... .	C. & E...	Olds	[illegible] Fri. 8.00.
Sunland..........	14	Victoria .	N B. & E	[illegible]am	Mon. Th. 7.00.
Suniebend.........	21	Edmonton..	Edmonton..	Pembina.	[illegible]. 8.00.
Sunnybrook.. .	20	Strathcona	C. & E	Leduc	Thors[illegible] Thur. 15.00.
Sunnydale.........	15f	Med. Hat......	S. & C......	. Excel.... .	Mon. Thu. ~~8.00~~.
Sunnynook......	17	Med. Hat......	~~Bassano~~.... Richdale...		M[illegible] F. 8.00.
Sunnyslope.........	17c	Red Deer.....	Calgary........	Acme...... ..	T. T. S. 8.00.
Swallowhurst.......	21	Edmonton.....	Edmonton....	Westlock... .	Mon. Fri. 15.00.

OFFICE	[illegible] No.	[illegible]TY	DISTRIBUTION	

OFFICE	KEY No.	COUNTY	DISTRIBUTION		
Swalwell	17c	Med. Hat	Calgary		L [illegible] 11, G.T.P
			Edmonton		Dy. tr. 1[illegible] G.T.P.
Sylvan Lake	20	Red Deer	C. & E.	Red Deer	M. [illegible] 61[illegible], C.P.R.

OFFICE	KEY No.	COUNTY	DISTRIBUTION		

OFFICE	KEY No.	COUNTY	DISTRIBUTION		
Taber...............	17	Med. Hat.....	M. H. & N. (1).	....	Dy. *tr 513, 514. Dy. trs 11, 512.
Talbot.............	14d	Red Deer......	C. & L.........	Coronation....	M. W. F. 1[illegible] 30.
Tarves.............	17	Med. Hat......	M. J. & C....	Walsh.....	Fri. 13.00.
Tawatinaw.........	21	Edmonton..	Edmonton.....	....	M. W. F. tr. 165, C.N.R.
Taylorville...... ..	18a	Med. Hat....	Lethbridge....	Cardston.	Tue. Sat. 14.00.
Telfordville........	20	Strathcona.. .	C. & E... ...	Leduc...	Calmar, Wed. Sat. 14 00.
Tees.	14d	Red Deer....	C. & L........		Dy. trs 529, 530.
Tempest.....	24	Red Deer....	S. & H.. .	Provost .	[illegible] 7.00.
The Gap......	17	Calgary ...	C. & V. (No. 1)	. ..	Dy. tr. 1.
Thelma....... ..	17	Med. Hat....	M. J. & C.	Irvine ...	Tue. Fri. 7 00.
Therien........	14	Victoria..	Vegreville	St. Paul de Metis. .. .	T. T. S. 14.00.
Thompson...	~~17~~	Med. Hat.....	M. H. & N. (1).	Seven Persons.	Tue. Fri. 7.00.
Thorhild.....	~~14~~	~~Victoria~~...	~~Fort Sask'n~~....	Radway Centre	Sat. 11 30.
Thorsby..... ..	20	Strathcona....	C. & E.......	Leduc.....	Buford, M. Th. 10.30.
Three Hills.........	17c	Red Deer....	Calgary..... Edmonton...	..	[illegible] 11, G.T.P. [illegible] 12, G.T.P.
Throne.....	29	~~Red Deer~~..	Coronation.. Kerr Robert..	.. .	M. W. F. tr. 612, C.P.R. T. T. S. tr 611, C.P.R.
Tide Lake..	17	Med. Hat.....	M. J. & C..	Alderson.	Tue. Fri. 14 00.
Tilly Station...	17	Med. Hat....	M. J. & C..	....	Dy. trs. 3, 4.
Tinchebray..... ..	14d	Red Deer.....	C. & L. . .	Castor ..	Tue. [illegible].00.
Tod Creek...... .	18	Macleod.	M. H. & N	Lundbreck..	Mon. 14.00.
Tofield...........	22b	Strathcona...	Edmonton.. W. & E..... Camrose.. ..	. . .	Dy. [illegible] 1[illegible], G.T.P. Dy. trs 1, 2. Dy. tr. 11, G.T.P.
Tolland...........	14	Strathcona...	T. B. & E.	Borradaile....	Tue Fri. 7.00.
Tollerton...... ...	30a	Edmonton..	Ed. & P. G.	Edson.	T. T. S. 9.00.
Tolman...........	26	~~Red Deer~~.....	Mun. & Cam..	Rumsey. ..	Thu. 14.30.
Tomahawk....... .	30a	Edmonton.....	Ed. & P. G....	Gainford......	Tue. Sat. 7.00.
Tongue Creek.. .	19	Macleod.......	Mac. & Cal.. ~~Calgary~~....	High River. ..	Tue. Sat. 7.00.
Topland...........	21	Edmonton....	Edmonton.....	~~Clyde~~........	[illegible]eman Riv Thur. 8.00.

OFF:	K.Y N.	UNTY	DISTRIBUTION

Office	Key No.	County	Distribution		
Travers....	17	Med. Hat...	~~Suffield Sta.~~		[illegible] 6[illegible] [illegible].P
Trenville....	17c	Red Deer....	Calgary... Edmonton..	Lousana	Mon. Th[illegible] 16.00
Tring....	14	Victoria....	N. B. & E.	Kitscoty....	Mon. Thur. 9.00.
Tripola....	17	Med. Hat....	Suffield [illegible]		Fri 7 [illegible]
Tristram....	14d	Red Deer....	[illegible]	[illegible]e.	Mon. Fri. 14 [illegible]0.
Trochu....	17c	Red Deer....	Calgary... Edmonton...	[illegible]	D[illegible] tr 11, [illegible] T.P. [illegible] 12 T.P.
Tudor....	17	~~Med. Hat~~....	Bassano...		[illegible] 7 [illegible]
Turin....	18a	Med. Hat....	Lethbridge...		Tue. Thu. Fri. Sat. 7.0[illegible]
Twin Butte....	18	Macleod....	M. H. & N....	Pincher Cr[illegible]ek.	Tu[illegible] [illegible] 8.00.
Twining...	17c	Red Deer....	Calgary....		Dy [illegible] 11, T[illegible]
Two Hills....	14	Victoria....	Vegreville...		M. W. F. [illegible]8.00.

OFFICE	KEY No.	COUNTY	DISTRIBUTION	

Office	Key No.	County	Distrib. tion		
Usona.............	20	Strathcona.....	C. & E.........	Ponoka.....	00.

Office	Key No.	County	Distribution		

Office	Key No.	County	Distribution		
Vale	17	Med. Hat	~~M. L. & C.~~	Pashley	[illegible] 9.00.
Vandyne	15t	Med. Hat	S. & C.	Alsask	Acadia Valle[illegible] Wed. Sat. 13.00.
Vanesti	14	Strathcona	N. B. & E.	Kitscoty	Tue. Fri. 8.00.
Vanrena	21	[illegible]dmonton	Edmonton	Pe[illegible]ce R. Crow	Wed. Sat. 8.00.
*Vegreville	14	Victoria	Edmonton N. B. & E. Camrose		D[illegible] tr. [illegible] D[illegible] *trs. 1, 2. M. W. F. tr. 1[illegible] C[illegible]
Veillette	14	Victoria	N. B. & E.	Lamont	[illegible]cred Heart, Tue. F. 14.00.
Verdant Valle[illegible]	15t	Med. Hat	S. & C.	Mecheche	Wed. 1[illegible]
*Vermilion	14	Victo[illegible]	[illegible] B. Edmonton		Dy* trs. 1, 2. D[illegible] t[illegible] 1[illegible] [illegible] R.
Vetchland	[illegible]	Red Deer	Red De[illegible]	[illegible] Mt.	[illegible]00.
Veteran		Red Deer	Coronation [illegible]		M. W. [illegible] tr. 61 [illegible] R. [illegible] tr. 511 [illegible]
Victor	15f	Red Deer	S. & C.	Craigmyle	Tue Fri. [illegible]00.
Viking	22b	[illegible]hcona	[illegible] & E.		Dy. trs. 1, 2.
Villeneuve	21	Edmonton	Edmonton	[illegible]. Albert	M. W. F. 10.30.
Vinca	14	Victoria	[illegible]		Tue. Fri. 8.00.
Vollmer	21	Edmonton	Edmonton		M. V[illegible] tr. 16 [illegible] N.R
Vulcan	17c	Macleod	Calgary Lethbridge		[illegible] tr. 1[illegible] C[illegible] [illegible] 511 [illegible]

OFFIC	K EY No.	COUNTY	DISTRIBUTION	

OFFICE	KEY No.	COUNTY	DISTRIBUTION		
Wabamun..........	30	Edmonton.....	Ed. & P. G. (1).	....	Mon. Thur. tr. 1. T. T. [illegible] tr. 4. Wed. [illegible] 2. Mon. [illegible] Tue [illegible] 91.
Wabasca...........	21	Edmonton.....	Edmonton....	[illegible]ridge..	2nd Mon each month.
Waddington........	17	Med. Hat......	M. J. & C..	[illegible]ashley.......	Mon. 9.00.
Wahstao...........	14	Victoria.......	N B. & E.	Lamont........	Wasel, Tue. Fri. 8.00.
Wainwright........	22a	Strathcona.....	W. & E..... Riv. & Wain.	....	Dy.[illegible] 2. Dy.* tr. 1.
Walsh.............	17	Med. Hat.....	M. J. & C.		[illegible]
Wanekville........	21	Edmonton....	Edmonton..	[illegible]rudo.	11.0[illegible]
Warner............	18a	Med. Hat...	Lethbridg[illegible]		[illegible]4, C.P.R.
Warwick...........	14	Victoria......	Vegreville......	....	Da[illegible]y 8.00.
Wasel.............	14	Victoria.......	N. B. & E.	Lamont........	Mon. Th. 7.00.
Wastina...........	15f	Red Deer......	Youngstown....	....	Tu[illegible] Fri. 13.00.
Water Glen........	20	Red Deer......	C. & E..	Ponoka ..	M. W. F 7.00.
Waterhole.........	21	Edmonton.....	Edmonton..	Peace R. Cross	Wed. Sat. 8.00.
Waterton Mills.....	18a	Med. Hat......	Lethbridge.....	Cardston.....	Moun[illegible] V[illegible] Tue. [illegible] 13.00.
Wattsford..........	14	Victoria. .	Vegreville. ..		Dy 8.00.
Waugh............	21	Edmonton...	Edmonton..	Clyde..	Mon. Fri. 13.30.
Wavy Lake.... ...	22b	Strathcona.....	W. & E......	Viking.	Tu[illegible]. Fri. 13.30
Waybrooke........	21	Edmonton....	Edmonton.. ..	Legal.........	Tue. Sat. 12.00.
Wayne..	15f	Med. Hat.. ..	S. & C.		[illegible] tr. 34 [illegible] Mon. tr. [illegible]
Wealthy..........	14	Victoria.......	N. B. & E.	Ma[illegible]ville....	7.00.
Welling...........	18a	Med. Hat......	Lethbridge...		Dy. tr. [illegible] C.P.R.
Wellsdale.........	14	Victoria.....	N. B. & E...	Islay.... ...	Dewberry, Tue. Fri. 13.00
Wellsville.........	18	Macleod.......	Macleod......	....	Tue. Fri. 14.00.
Wenham Valley....	24	Strathcona.....	Wetaskiwin...	Yeoford......	Mon. Fri. 11.00.
Weno............	17c	Calgary.......	Calgary........	....	Dy. 8.00.
Wessington........	26	Red Deer..	Mun. & Cam.	Red Willow...	Wed. Sat. 14.30.

Office	Key No.	County	Distribution	

Office	Key No.	Cou[illegible]		Di[illegible]	
Westerdale...	20	Red Deer.....	C. & E...	Olds..	[illegible] 12 00.
Westerose......	24	[illegible]trathcona....	[illegible]		
Westlock.	21	Edmonton. ..	Edmont[illegible]	[illegible]	[illegible]
W[illegible]t Pe[illegible]	21	[illegible]nto[illegible]	[illegible]		
West Salisbury	[illegible]0	[illegible]			
Westward H[illegible]	[illegible]0	R[illegible]r.			1. 0[illegible]
West Wing	1[illegible]	Red Deer. ..	[illegible]		[illegible]
*W[illegible]etas[illegible]in.	[illegible]	[illegible]tr[illegible]ona			
What[illegible]	1[illegible]	Red [illegible]	[illegible]		[illegible]
Wh[illegible] C[illegible]nt[illegible]	17	M[illegible] H[illegible]	[illegible] Sta		[illegible]
White Court.. ..	[illegible]	Edmonton.			
Whitefish Lake.	14	[illegible]ctoria .	V[illegible]ville	Du[illegible]	
Whitford... .	14	Victo[illegible]			[illegible] T[illegible] Fri. 8.00.
Whitla... . .	17	Med. Hat..	M. H. [illegible] N. 1[illegible]	.	[illegible]11, 51[illegible]
Whitton....		Red Deer.	[illegible] ob[illegible]rt	[illegible]	.. 12[illegible]
Wien... .. .	21	Edmonton..	[illegible]monton		[illegible]00 .
Wildmere.. . .	14	Strathcona...	[illegible]	[illegible]	
Wildunn......	[illegible]	Med. Hat.. .	& C... .	[illegible]	[illegible] 14.00
Wilhelmina. .	[illegible]	Red Deer.	[illegible]		[illegible] T. [illegible]
Willesden Green..	20	Red D[illegible]	C. & E .	Ponoka .	[illegible]a, Sat. 1[illegible]30.
Wilton Park.....	20	Strathcon[illegible]	& E...	Ledu[illegible].	[illegible]
Wimborne..... .	20	Red Deer.. .	C. & E ..	Old[illegible]	[illegible]day[illegible]n, Tu[illegible] Fri. 14.00.
Winnifred........	17	Med. Hat....	M. H. & N. (1[illegible] ..		[illegible] 513, 51[illegible]
Winnington..... .	17	Med. Ha[illegible]	[illegible]a[illegible] o.. Empre[illegible]	[illegible]	[illegible] T. [illegible]00.
Winterburn... .	21	Edmonton...	[illegible]monton...	.... .	[illegible]. T. [illegible] 15
Wisdom.. ..	17	Med. Hat.....	Medicine Hat..	Rosebeg......	Fri. 14.00.

OFFICE	KEY No.	COUNTY	DISTRIBUTION		

OFFICE	KEY No.	COUNTY	DISTRIBUTION		
Wiste............	29	Red Deer.....	Coronation.. Kerr Robert..	Loyalist......	Mon. Fri. 12.00.
Wittenburg........	20	Red Dee[illegible]	[illegible]mbe......	Bentley........	Wed. 7.00, Sat. 12.30.
Wolf Creek........	30a	Edmonton.....	Ed. & P. G..........	....	Mon. Thur. tr. 1. T. T. S. trs. 3, 4. Wed. Sat. tr. 2. Mon. tr. 92, Tue. tr. 91.
Woodbend.........	21	Edmonton.....	Edmonton......	....	Fri. 14.30.
Woodglen.........	22b	Strathcona....	W. & E........	Viking.........	Tue. Fri. 13.30
Wood River........	20	Red Deer......	C. & E.........	Ponoka........	M. W. F. 7.00.
Woolchester.......	17	Med. Hat.....	Medicine Hat..	....	Tue. Fri. 7.45.
Woolford Station...	18a	Med. Hat......	Lethbridge.....	Cardston......	Tue. Fri. 11.30
Wostok...........	14	Victoria.......	N. B. & E.....	Lamont.......	Mon. Th. 7.00.
Wrentham.........	18a	Med. Hat......	Lethbridge.....	New Dayton...	Wed. Sat. 12.30

OFFICE	KEY No.	COUNTY	DISTRIBUTION	

OFFICE	KEY No.	COUNTY	DISTRIBUTION		
Yates...........	[illegible]0[illegible]	Edmonton.....	Ed. [illegible] P. [illegible]	[illegible]	[illegible] 4. T[illegible] tr. [illegible]
Yeoford.. ...	[illegible]4	Strathcona.	[illegible]etaskiwin..	[illegible] ..	. T. [illegible]00
Yetwood.........	17[illegible]	Med. Hat...	Lethbridge.. / Calgary....	[illegible]hampion..	Tue. Fri. 1[illegible].00.
Youngstown... ...	1[illegible]	Med. Hat...	[illegible]. & C...	[illegible]	D[illegible] [illegible] [illegible]3-24.
Yule Meadow..	20	Strathcona..	C. & F....	[illegible]illet......	[illegible] 00

OFFICE	KEY No.	COUNTY	DISTRIBUTION		

Office	Key No.	County	Distribution		
Zawale..........	14	Victoria.......	N. B. & E.....	Lamont.......	Andrew, Tue. Fri. 8.00.
Zenith..........	14d	Red Deer......	C. & L........	Botha.	Fri. 8.00.
Zetland..........	20	Red Deer......	Coronation... K [illegible]	Veteran.. ..	[illegible] Sat. 10.35.
Zoldovara........ 22a	[illegible]	~~Strathcona~~....	W. & E.. (1).	Irma........	Fri. 14 00.

ALPHABETICAL LIST OF PLACES IN WESTERN ONTARIO SHOWING DESPATCH OF EACH FROM WINNIPEG STANDPOINT. THESE PLACES ARE KEYED TO THE FOLLOWING SIX SEPARATIONS:—

1.—Ft. Fr[illegible]d Winnipeg R.P.O.
2.—Ft. William and Winnipeg R.P.O.
3.—Port Arthur.
4.—Fort William.
5.—Winnipeg District.
x2.—Sudbury & Ft. William.

NOTE.—Points in brackets ( ) are non-Post Offices.

K. No		[illegible]t.	Distribution.

ALPHABETICAL LIST OF PLACES IN WESTERN ONTARIO SHOWING DISPATCH OF EACH FROM WINNIPEG STANDPOINT. THESE PLACES ARE KEY[illegible]D TO THE FOLLOWING SIX SEPARATIONS:—

1.—Ft. Frances and Winnipeg R.P.O.
2.—Ft. William and Winnipeg R.P.O.
3.—Port Arthur.
4.—Fort William.
5.—Winnipeg Di[illegible]
x2.—Sudbury & Ft. [illegible]illia[illegible]

NOTE.—Points in brackets ( ) [illegible] non-Post Off[illegible]

KEY NO.	OFFICE	DISTRICT	D[illegible]
1	Atikokan.... ...	T. B. & R. [illegible]	[illegible] [illegible] [illegible]thu [illegible]
x2	Aviemoor..	Algoma.	
1	Aylesworth...	T. B. [illegible] R. R.	[illegible]
4	Baird...	T. B. & R. R.	
2	(Barclay Siding).. .	.. ..	[illegible]
1	Banning... ...	T. B. & R. R.	[illegible] [illegible]an[illegible]es. W[illegible]li[illegible]m [illegible] [illegible]thur
1	Barnhart.. . ..	T. B. & R. R.	[illegible]
1	Barwick...	T. B. & R. R..	
2	(Bears Pass)	. . ..	[illegible] F[illegible]
2	Bedworth..	T. B. & R. R	
2	(Begsley)...	. . .	[illegible] [illegible]on.
1	Bergland..	T. B. & R. R	. [illegible]
1	Big Fork.....	T. B. [illegible] R. R.	.. [illegible] lin.
2	(Biota).....	. . . .	[illegible]
x2	Biscotasing......... .	Algoma .	
1	Black Hawk....... .	T. B. & R. R	. [illegible]
2	Bonheur..	T. B. [illegible] R. R..	
1	Boucherville...	T. B. & R. R.. ..	[illegible]on Stn.
1	Box Alder.... . . .	T. B. & R. R.. ...	De[illegible]li[illegible]
2	(Braid)....	.. ...	[illegible]
2	(Brule Stn).......	. . . ..	Din[illegible]rwic.
2	(Buda)...................	. .. .	K[illegible]kwia.
1	Burris........	T. B. & R. R....	Devlin.
2	(Butler)..	....	[illegible]gnace.

ALPHABETICAL LIST OF PLACES IN WESTERN ONTARIO SHOWING DESPATCH OF EAST FROM WINNIPEG STANDPOINT. THESE PLACES ARE KEYED TO THE FOLLOWING SIX SEPARATIONS:—

1.—Ft. Frances and Winnipeg R.P.O.
2.—Ft. William and Winnipeg R.P.O
3.—Port Arthur.
4.—Fort William.
5.—Winnipeg District.
x2.—Sudbury & Ft. William.

NOTE.—Points in brackets ( ) are non-Post Offices.

Key No.	Office.	District.	Distribution.

ALPHABETICAL LIST OF PLACES IN WESTERN ONTARIO SHOWING DESPATCH OF EACH FROM WINNIPEG STANDPOINT. THESE PLACES ARE KEYED TO THE FOLLOWING SIX SEPARATIONS:—

1.—Ft. Frances and Winnipeg R.P.O.
2.—Ft. William and Winnipeg R.P.O.
3.—Port Arthur.
4.—Ft. William.
5.—Winnipeg Dis.
x2.—Sudbury & Ft. William.

NOTE.—Points in brackets ( ) are non-Post Offices.

KEY NO.	OFFICE.	DISTRICT.	DISTRIBUTION.
1	(Calm Lake)		Ft. Frances. Pt. Arthur.
x2	Chapleau	Algoma.	
1	Chapple	T. B. & R. R.	Barwick.
3	Cloud Bay	T. B. & R. R.	
4 or 3	Conmee	T. B. & R. R.	
1	Crozier	T. B. & R. R.	
2	(Dagero)		
1	Dearlock	T. B. & R. R.	Barwi
1	Dermid	T. B. & R. R.	Devlin.
1	Devlin	T. B. & R. R.	
2	(Dexter)		
2	Dinorwic	T. B. & R. R.	
x2	Dorion Station	T. B. & R. R.	
2	Dryden	T. B. & R. R.	
2	Dyment	T. B. & R. R.	
2	(Eagle River)		Vermilion Bay.
2	(Edison)		
4	Ellis	T. B. & R. R.	
1	Emo	T. B. & R. R.	
2	English	T. B. & R. R.	
x2	Everard	T. B. & R. R.	
2	(Falcon)		Ignace.
3	Farrington	T. B. & R. R.	Port Arthur.
1	Finland	T. B. & R. R.	Barwick.
2	(Finmark)		Kaministikwia.
x2	Fitzbach	Algoma, W. R.	Franz.

ALPHABETICAL LIST OF PLACES IN WESTERN ONTARIO SHOWING DESPATCH OF EAST FROM WINNIPEG STANDPOINT. THESE PLACES ARE KEYED TO THE FOLLOWING SIX SEPARATIONS:—

1.—F[illegible]nce and Winnipeg R.P.O.
2.—Ft. William and Winnipeg R.P.O.
3.—Port Arthur.
4.—Fort William.
5.—Winnipeg District.
x2.—Sudbury & Ft. William.

NOTE.—Points in brackets ( ) are non-Po[illegible] Offi[illegible]s.

No.	Office.	District.	Distribution.

ALPHABETICAL LIST OF PLACES IN WESTERN ONTARIO SHOWING DESPATCH OF EACH FROM WINNIPEG STANDPOINT. THESE PLACES ARE KEYED TO THE FOLLOWING SIX SEPARATIONS:—

1.—Ft. Frances and Winnipeg R.P.O.
2.—Ft. William and Winnipeg R.P.O.
3.—Port Arthur.
4.—Ft. William.
5.—Winnipeg Dis.
x2.—Sudbury & Ft. William.

NOTE.—Points in brackets ( ) are n n-Post Offi

KEY No.	OFFICE	DIS RICT	
3	Flint........	T. B. & R. R...	
1	Fort Franc s.	T. B R R.	
2	Fort W illiam..	T. B. & R. R..	
2	Ft. William West....	R.	5.
x2	Franz.		
1	Gameland..........	F	
2	(Guilbert)............		
1	(Glenorchy)......		
2	Gold Rock.....	T. B. R.	W
2	(Good Lake)..........		
4	(Grassey)......		
2	(Gull River)..........		I
2	Hawk Lake....	B R. R..	
x2	Heron Bay......	T. B. & R. R...	
3	(Huronian)		
3	Hymers..........	T. B. & R. R	
2	Ignace.........	T. B. & R.	
2	Ingolf......	T. B. & R. R	
3	Intola......	T. B. & R. R...	
1	Isherwood..........	T. B. & R. R....	rozier.
x2	Jackfish...	T. B. & R. R..	
1	Jual..................	T. B. & R. R.........	De n.
3	Kakabeka Falls............	T. B. & R. R........	Port Arthur. t. William. Ft. Frances.
2	(Kalmar)..................		
2	Kaministikwia..............	T. B. & R. R............	

ALPHABETICAL LIST OF PLACES IN WESTERN ONTARIO SHOWING DESPATCH OF EACH FROM WINNIPEG STANDPOINT. THESE PLACES ARE KEYED TO THE FOLLOWING SIX SEPARATIONS:—

1.—Ft. Frances and Winnipeg R.P.O.
2.—Ft. William and Winnipeg R.P.O.
3.—Port Arthur.
4.—Fort William.
5.—Winnipeg District.
x2.—Sudbury & Ft. William.

NOTE.—Points in brackets ( ) are non-Post Offices.

Key No.	Office.	District.	Distribution.

ALPHABETICAL LIST OF PLACES IN WESTERN ONTARIO SHOWING DESPATCH OF EACH FROM WINNIPEG STANDPOINT. THESE PLACES ARE KEYED TO THE FOLLOWING SIX SEPARATIONS:—

1.—Ft. Frances and Winnipeg R.P.O.
2.—Ft. William and Winnipeg R.P.O.
3.—Port Arthur.
4.—Ft. William.
5.—Winnipeg Di[illegible]
x2.—Sudbury & Ft. William

NOTE—Points in brackets [illegible] n-Post Offices

KEY No.	OFFICE	DISTRICT	DISTRIBUTION
1	Kashabowie	T. B. & R. R.	Ft. Frances. Pt. Arthur. Ft. William
3	Kawene	T. B. & R. R.	
2	Keewatin	T. B. & R. R.	
2	Kenora	T. B. & R.	

ALPHABETICAL LIST OF PLACES IN WESTERN ONTARIO SHOWING DESPATCH OF EACH FROM WINNIPEG STANDPOINT. THESE PLACES ARE KEYED TO THE FOLLOWING SIX SEPARATIONS:—

1.—Ft. Frances and Winnipeg R.P.O.
2.—Ft. William and Winnipeg R.P.O.
3.—Port Arthur.
4.—Fort William.
5.—Winnipeg District.
x2.—Sudbury & Ft. William.

NOTE.—Points in brackets ( ) are non-Post Offices.

Key No.	Office.	District	Distribution.

ALPHABETICAL LIST OF PLACES IN WESTERN ONTARIO SHOWING DESPATCH OF EACH FROM WINNIPEG STANDPOINT. THESE PLACES ARE KEYED TO THE FOLLOWING SIX SEPARATIONS:—

1.—Ft. Frances and Winnipeg R.P.O.
2—Ft. William and Winnipeg R.P.O.
3.—Port Arthur.
4.—Ft. William.
5.—Winnipeg Dist.
x2.—Sudbury & Ft. William.

Note.—Points in brackets ( ) are non-Post Offices.

Key No.	Office	District	Distribution
1	Mine Cent. Station.	T. B. & R. R.	Ft. Frances. Ft. William. Pt. Arthur.
2	Minnitaki	T. B. & R. R.	
x2	Missanabie	Algoma	
3	Moose Hill	T. B. & R. R.	
1	Morson.	T. B. & R. R.	Sleeman.
2	Murillo..	T. B. & R. R..	
x2	Nemegos.	Algoma.	
x2	Nicholson Siding..	Algoma..	
x2	Nepigon..	T. B. & R. R..	
2	(Niblock)		Savanne.
1	(Nickle Lake		Fort Frances.
3	Nolalu.	T. &. & R. R..	
2	Norman....	T. B. & R. R.	
1	North Branch.	T. B. & R. R...	Stratton Station.
4	(North EastBay)		
5 or 4	North Pines.	T. B. & R. R.	
4	(O'Brien)..		
3	O'Connor..	T. B. & R. R.	
1	(Olive)...		Ft. Frances.
2	(Osaquan).		Ignace.
x2	Ouimet...	T. B. & R. R.	
2	Oxdrift.	T. B. & R. R.	
2	(Parry)......		Vermilion Bay.
1	Patullo....	T. B. & R. R.	Stratton Station.
x2	Pine.........	Algoma..........	

ALPHABETICAL LIST OF PLACES IN WESTERN ONTARIO SHOWING DESPATCH OF EACH FROM WINNIPEG STANDPOINT. THESE PLACES ARE KEYED TO THE FOLLOWING SIX SEPARATIONS:—

1. Ft. Frances and Winnipeg R.P.O.
2. Ft. William and Winnipeg R.P.O.
3. Port Arthur.
4.—Fort William.
5.—Winnipeg District.
x2.—Sudbury & Ft. William.

NOTE.—Points in brackets ( ) are non-Post Offices

Key No.	Office.	District.	Distribution.

ALPHABETICAL LIST OF PLACES IN WESTERN ONTARIO SHOW[illegible]G DESPATCH [illegible] EACH FRO[illegible] WINNIPEG STANDPOINT. THE[illegible] PLACES ARE [illegible]EYED TO T[illegible] FOLLOWIN[illegible] SIX SEPA[illegible]TIONS:—

1.—Ft. Frances and W[illegible]nipeg R.P.C [illegible] Willi[illegible]
2.—Ft. William and Winnipeg R.P[illegible]). [illegible] Winnipeg D[illegible]
3.—Port Arthur. [illegible]—Sudbury & Ft. Willia[illegible]

N[illegible]—P[illegible] in bracke[illegible] re non-Post Offic[illegible]

KEY NO	C[illegible]	DISTR[illegible]	DISTRIBU[illegible]TIO[illegible]
1	Pin[illegible]	T. B. & R. [illegible]	
2	(Polan[illegible]		S[illegible]vann[illegible].
2	Port A[illegible]	T. B & R R	
x2	Port Cold[illegible]ll	T. [illegible]. & R. R.	
x2	Pulp Siding..	Algon[illegible]	
5	Quibell..	T. B. & R R	Vermilion Bay.
1	Rainy River.	T. B. & R. R.	
2	Rai[illegible]h.	T. B & R. R	
2	(Raleigh		T[illegible]ch Sta[illegible]ion.
x2	Rams[illegible]	Algon[illegible]	
1	Rapid River.	T B & R. R	Ra[illegible] River
[illegible]or 4	Richan.	T. B. & R. R. ..	Sioux Lookout
1	(Rocky Inlet		Fort France[illegible]
3	(Rosslyn Village..	T B. R.	
x2	Rossport	T. B. & [illegible]. R	
x2	Ruel...	Algo[illegible]	
4	St. Anthony Mine.	T B. R .	
1	Sannes...	T B. & [illegible]. R.	[illegible]le man.
2	Savanne...	T. B. & R. R.	
x[illegible]	[illegible]chreiber.	T. B. & R. R.... ..	
2	(Scovil)		Vermilion Ba[illegible]
3	Sella	T B. & R. R.............	
3	(Sha		
2	[illegible]heb.		Savanne.
1	Shenston.	T. B. & R. R.	Stratton Sta[illegible]
4 or 5	[illegible]oux Look[illegible]	T. B. & R. R........ ..	

ALPHABETICAL LIST OF PLACES IN WESTERN ONTARIO SHOWING DESPATCH OF EACH FROM WINNIPEG STANDPOINT. THESE PLACES ARE KEYED TO THE FOLLOWING SIX SEPARATIONS:—

1.—Ft. Frances and Winnipeg R.P.O.
2.—Ft. William and Winnipeg R.P.O.
3.—Port Arthur.
4.—Fort William.
5.—Winnipeg District.
x2.—Sudbury & Ft. William.

NOTE.—Points in brackets ( ) are non-Post Offices.

Key No.	Office.	District.	Distribution.

ALPHABETICAL LIST OF PLACES IN WE [illegible] TARI[illegible] EACH FROM WINNIPEG STANDPOINT Th[illegible] R [illegible] FOLLOWING SIX [illegible]EP[illegible] ATION[illegible]

1.—Ft. Frances and Winnipeg R.P.O.
2.—Ft. William and Winnipeg R.P.O.
3.—Port Arthur

4 [illegible] Willi[illegible]
Winnipeg [illegible]
[illegible] Sudbury [illegible]

Note.—Points in bracket [illegible] on-P[illegible]

Key No.	[illegible]	Di[illegible]	[illegible]
or 4	[illegible] I[illegible]	T. B. & R. R.	
	[illegible] Mount[illegible]	T. B. & R. R.	
[illegible]	[illegible]la[illegible] Riv[illegible] [illegible]ll[illegible]	T. B. & R. R.	
1	[illegible]lee[illegible]	T. B. & R. R.	
[illegible]	[illegible] ll[illegible]		[illegible]
	[illegible]outh [illegible]lli	T. B. & R. R.	
3 or 4	[illegible]tanle[illegible]	T. B. & R. R.	
1	[illegible]p Roc[illegible]		[illegible]
1	[illegible]ton.	T. B. & R. R.	
4	[illegible]rgeon La[illegible]	T. B. & R. R.	
4	Superior Ju[illegible]t[illegible]n	T. B. & R. R.	
2	Ta[illegible]h[illegible] [illegible]atio[illegible]	T. B. [illegible] R.	
2	Tam[illegible]		[illegible]
x2	Trudeau.	T. B. & R. R.	
1	Turtl[illegible]		[illegible]
2	Upsala		[illegible]
2	Vermilion Bay....	T. B. & R. R.	
2	Wabigoon.	[illegible]	
5	Wade		
4	Wako.	[illegible] R.	
2	Waldho[illegible] ...	T. B. & R. R.	
3	Wamsl[illegible]	[illegible]	
x2	Wayl[illegible]	[illegible]lgon[illegible]	
x2	White Ri[illegible]r....	[illegible]. B.	
x2	Windy L[illegible]	[illegible]lg[illegible]m	

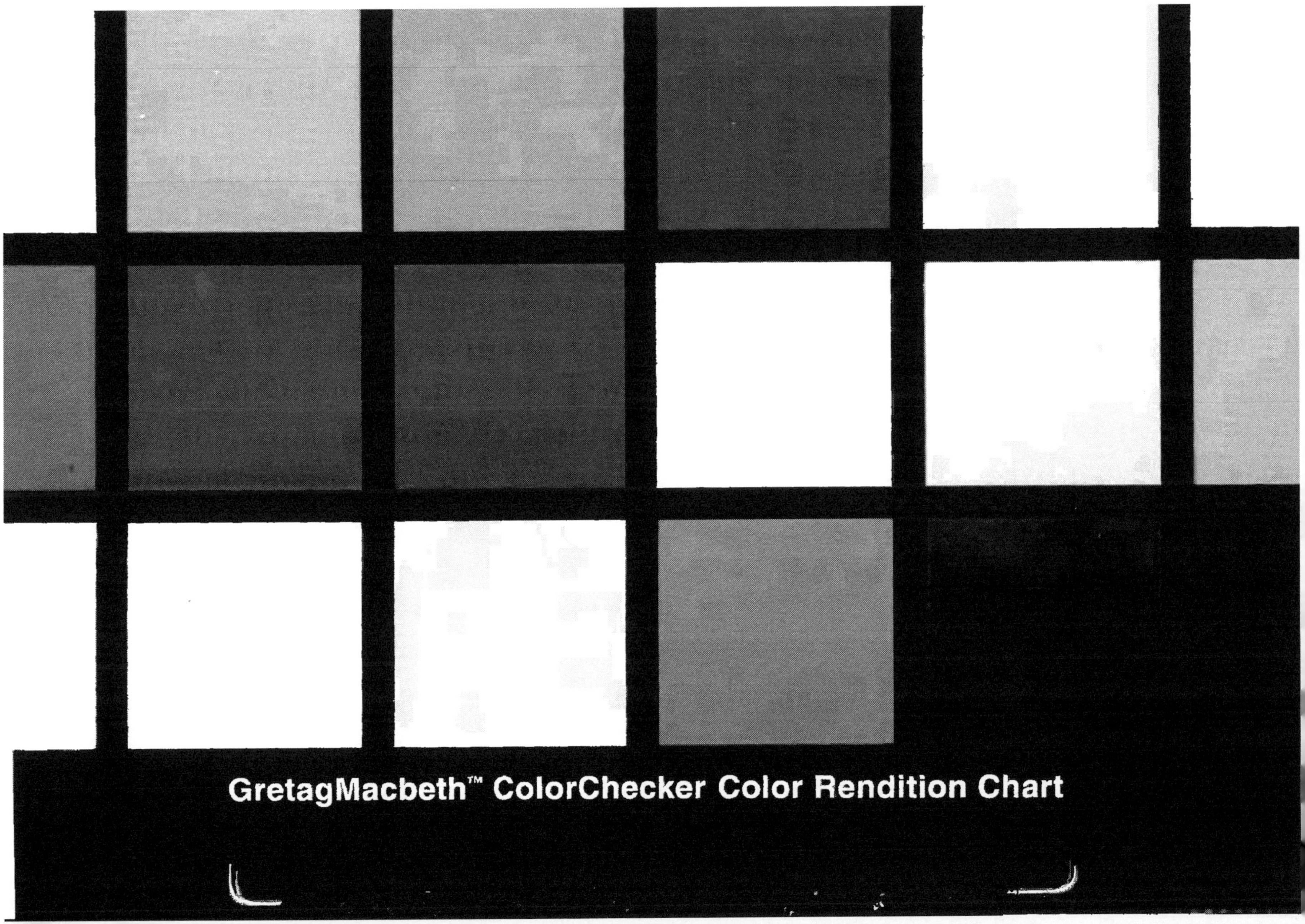

GretagMacbeth™ ColorChecker Color Rendition Chart

Lightning Source UK Ltd.
Milton Keynes UK
UKHW031832070920
369495UK00008B/1824